BIG BOOK PAYOFFS

BIG BOOK PAYOFFS

WHY EVERY ENTREPRENEUR SHOULD WRITE A BOOK

(AND HOW TO DO IT)

DAN SULLIVAN
AND TUCKER MAX

LIONCREST
PUBLISHING

BIG BOOK PAYOFFS

Why Every Entrepreneur Should Write a Book (and How to Do It)

ISBN   978-1-5445-1704-9 *Hardcover*

       978-1-5445-1705-6 *Paperback*

       978-1-5445-1706-3 *Ebook*

TO ALL THE RISK TAKERS AND ENTREPRENEURS,

THIS BOOK IS FOR YOU.

CONTENTS

WHY READ THIS BOOK?

Dan Sullivan has a rule:

> *I never try to sell something I'm not sold on. I only sell things that I truly believe are good for the other person.*

Considering that he's written 55 books (as of July 2020), Dan is sold on the benefits of writing a book. I'm helping Dan write this book because of a defining idea in his life (and mine):

Every single entrepreneur on earth should write a book because it's the best thing they can do for themselves, their business, and their team.

That's it—our cards are on the table. We wrote this book to convince every entrepreneur on earth to write a book, and to show them the fastest, simplest, and best way to do it.

If you're an entrepreneur who's already written your book(s), and you have a great process to write more (like Dan does), then stop reading.

If you aren't an entrepreneur—or aren't planning to be one ever—this book isn't for you either. I've written several other books on how to write a general nonfiction book or a memoir. You can read those (*The Scribe Method* is where to start) since they're more suited to someone who does not have the specific life circumstances of an entrepreneur and business owner.

But if you're an entrepreneur and you've been thinking about writing a book, *this is the book for you.*

In this book, you'll learn why the world's most successful entrepreneur coach (Dan Sullivan) recommends that every single one of his entrepreneur clients write a book.

We'll walk you through each and every benefit an entrepreneur can get from writing and publishing their book (you might think you know the reasons, but some will surprise you).

Then we'll help you ensure that writing a book makes sense for you by showing you how to sell yourself on writing a book—or not—before you start.

We'll detail precisely how to structure your book, so it's appealing to your audience and gets you the maximum possible impact.

We'll tell you all the tips and tricks we use to make the writing and editing as easy and fun as possible.

Then we'll tell you exactly how to publish the book (hint: hire someone to help you).

And we end by teaching you the basics and fundamentals of marketing your book and show you where most everyone gets this wrong (spoiler alert: the trick is to use the book to market you; that's where the biggest payoffs are.)

Let me warn you: **this book will teach you a perspective unlike anything you've ever read about writing a book.**

That's because most everything you've read on that topic was written by a professional writer, for other professional writers. What those professional writers teach is how to be better at performing the rituals that a professional writer needs to care about to fit into their profession.

But that's not you at all. You don't have to care about the silly things professional writers care about. You're an entrepreneur, and for you the book is a means to an end, not the end itself.

Things that matter to professional writers that don't matter to you:

- what desk to use for writing
- which software is best for writers
- which book agent is best
- which publishing company you have to impress to get a deal
- which writers' conferences to go to
- how to get coverage in *Publishers Weekly*

That's all irrelevant to you.

As an entrepreneur, you have different concerns.

You probably care first and foremost about your book being good for your readers (who are probably your customers).

Then you probably care about it representing you and your company well.

Then you probably want it to be something you are proud of and can show people to help them understand you better.

And unlike professional writers, you also don't have a lot of extra time, and you don't want to spend it on writing a book. You want your ideas to get onto the page and out into the world as fast as possible.

You don't want to learn how to be a professional writer—you just want to write a great book.

That's the primary difference between this book and all others about writing a book—it's written for YOU specifically as an entrepreneur.

Following along with that, the most important concept we will teach in this book—the thing we'll come back to again and again—is what Dan calls "Who Not How."

Instead of thinking, *How do I write this book?* we're going to show you a better frame for the question:

Who do I hire to help me write this book?

And whether you know it or not, you've already made your first hire: this book.

You're "hiring" this book to help you understand why to write your own book, how to do it easily, and how to use the book to get a big payoff—and you're skipping all the hard parts of learning this process yourself. You're buying decades of experience and wisdom to rocket yourself up the book-learning curve.

That's why I'm here. My name is Tucker Max, and I'm Dan's "Who" for this book.

I've been a writer for 20 years, written 4 *New York Times* bestsellers of my own that sold nearly 5 million copies worldwide, and over my career, I've advised or helped people like Tim Ferriss, Peter Thiel, Dave Asprey, and a slew of others with their books.

But more importantly, I'm also an entrepreneur. I started a company called Scribe Media to help busy, successful people write, publish, and market their books as quickly, easily, and effectively as possible (we, in fact, helped Dan on his book *Who Not How*, and that's how Dan and I got to know each other well).

Most of our clients are entrepreneurs, and to effectively work with them, we had to develop a new way to approach book writing. We couldn't just use the old-school "open a vein and bleed on your keyboard" approach.

We also couldn't do pure ghostwriting, either. Our clients wanted the book to be entirely their words and their ideas, even if we helped them with the writing.

It took a lot of pain and effort, but we eventually figured it out. Over the past 6 years, we've done close to 2,000 books, some of them with very famous and successful entrepreneurs.

You might've heard of David Goggins? We did his massive bestseller, *Can't Hurt Me*. Other clients include Nassim

Nicholas Taleb, Gino Wickman (EOS inventor), Kevin Harrington (original Shark on *Shark Tank*), David Bach (10x *New York Times* bestselling author), Janice Bryant Howroyd (entrepreneur and the first black woman to run a $1 billion enterprise), Whitney Tilson, Mark Divine, Shep Hyken, Tiffany Haddish, Todd Herman, Joey Coleman, and the Nobel Prize Committee (seriously).

Our clients have had books on the *New York Times* bestseller list, the *Wall Street Journal* bestseller list, and the *USA Today* bestseller list—about a dozen on those lists in total.

And our writing programs on ScribeBookSchool.com have helped tens of thousands of people (for free) to write and publish their books as well.

The point of telling you this is not to brag. You don't care what my company has done, nor should you.

The point is to help you understand why Dan picked us to work with, and why you might want to listen to what I'm telling you:

The process you're about to learn is specifically designed to help entrepreneurs just like you write and publish their books, and it is proven to work.

All you have to do is follow the steps and you'll get there, and

PART 1

WHY EVERY ENTREPRENEUR SHOULD WRITE A BOOK

Writing a book is a tremendous experience. It pays off intellectually. It clarifies your thinking. It builds credibility. It is a living engine of marketing and idea spreading, working every day to deliver your message with authority. You should write one.

—SETH GODIN

[If you're already certain that you want to write a book and are ready to start, you can skip to part 2.]

The most successful entrepreneurs think in terms of big payoffs and least amount of effort. In other words, the best entrepreneurs focus relentlessly on increasing productivity.

Why? Because Productivity multiplies Profitability, which, in turn, helps create more Productivity.

That's the one formula that differentiates entrepreneurs from non-entrepreneurs.

And *great* entrepreneurs are 100x better at growing this formula than mediocre ones (both Jeff Bezos and Elon Musk focus ruthlessly on it). That's why we titled this book *Big Book Payoffs*.

A book is one of the single best "unfair advantages" an entrepreneur can use to dominate a market and get a massive payoff.

So why doesn't every entrepreneur have a book?

Well, if you've never produced a book before, the effort can feel overwhelming, and the payoffs can seem uncertain at the beginning.

Why do the payoffs seem uncertain?

The payoffs of a book are spread across several different areas, and they are often hard to see directly until *after* you've published the book. Not to mention, they're often hard to quantify with numbers, so the bean counters never approve.

And, of course, the simplest way to measure payoffs is the one thing you should NOT worry about: sales.

The money you can make from book sales is a drop in the bucket compared to the money you can make from the many other payoffs a book provides.

But in my experience, entrepreneurs don't consider them as much as they look at their competition. They don't realize that the best "stories" are what sell, and that "context" is always 1,000x more persuasive than "content."

As a result, they often don't see that books create the greatest advantage with the least amount of effort.

BOOKS ARE MAGICAL

Books are magical. I mean that *almost* literally.

Think about it: you put your thoughts onto a screen (or paper) one time, and from that moment on, everyone on earth can know what you think.

And based off those written thoughts, they can decide to give you money, or work with you, or change their behavior, simply because of the ideas you wrote down once.

And this magic can last forever.

Most people today spend half a day every week asking for help and love and forgiveness from an invisible being they've never met, all because a Jewish carpenter 2,000 years ago told them this was their God, and then another guy wrote it all down.

I'm not criticizing Jesus or Christians, obviously, just pointing out that most of what we all believe comes from books.

This is incredible, magical leverage.

I grew up in a book culture, but I wouldn't call the culture that we're living in today a book culture. It's a media culture. It's an internet culture. It's a TV culture. It's an immediate-gratification culture for people who don't do hard work because "someone else" does it.

That's why you're a successful entrepreneur—you do the work others won't do, right?

Because of this culture, I believe books are even more magical now than they were in previous centuries. That's because the whole notion of someone writing a book has more magic today than it had even 25 or 30 years ago.

I can tell you from experience this is true. Every time I tell people what I do, the next statement out of their mouths is, "I've always wanted to write a book."

And then they stop talking.

Even though I literally own a company that helps people write and publish books, *very few actually ask me how to do it.*

You know why?

They're afraid.

Even though it's much easier to write a book and get it published these days, the notion that you're good enough to write a book—that you're special enough to write a book—still has a tremendous magic to it.

Most people know it's possible, but they don't believe THEY can do it.

Once you get past that barrier, it changes you, both in your eyes and in the eyes of others. You become the person who conquered the demon others couldn't face.

Books create a magical transformation. They provide countless benefits and last forever, creating an incredibly high return relative to the effort required to make them.

We've identified 19 total unique payoffs from writing a book that fall into 5 broad categories.

THE 19 UNIQUE PAYOFFS BOOKS CREATE FOR ENTREPRENEURS

1. PRESTIGE/BRAND PAYOFFS

Books are essential if you want to elevate your brand, authority, and prestige.

A Book Levels Up Your Identity

Before you write a book, you're just a regular person like anyone else. But after you write and publish your book, you have a new identity: you're an author.

You've made your ideas real, in a format that allows others to assess, analyze, and debate them—and that opens you up to the next level of learning and expansion.

In essence, your book becomes a magic bridge into a different identity.

This shift in identity moves you up a level in life. You're now in a different league, and you have a new peer group.

A book confirms that the work you do matters to other people, and it invites new dialogue and connection with a much larger audience.

Before the book, there's you as a one-on-one, face-to-face salesperson. But once you write a book, countless other mediums and media become possible for you and your brand. It can get you booked for interviews, podcasts, speeches, and so much more.

As a result, *you* get to choose which opportunities you want to take and who *you* want to work with.

Before you write your book, you're a seller. After you write it, you're a buyer.

And it's all because writing a book transforms your identity. It transforms how people think of you. Before the book, you are like them. After the book, you are something they are not, something very valuable: an author.

This new identity represents you in situations that you couldn't predict, and it creates dimensions of interest in the world that you would have never foreseen.

This identity gives you credibility with others. It connects you with like-minded people. It connects you with opportunities. And it propels you to your next level of capability and next level of confidence.

Every time you write a book, you take a jump in identity.

Joey Coleman is an excellent example. After releasing his book, *Never Lose a Customer Again*, Joey's inbox filled up with invitations from people who'd never even heard him speak before. He saw a *4x increase* in the number of speaking requests he got each month.

But one of his favorite opportunities came when the CEO of a billion-dollar European company wanted Joey to keynote the company's annual meeting—in just 3 weeks.

"It was the type of call where they're like, 'We read your book, we love it, and we're booking you. Just tell me how much it's going to cost.'

I've done plenty of keynotes, but never one like that, where they came to me with a blank check."

A Book Positions You in the World

I believe we can create most of our reality, and a book creates a reality where you can be regarded the way you want to be (assuming you've done enough work to get there, of course).

Your book tells the world *a story about who you are and how to regard you.* It's a form of self-packaging.

This is no different than the way you dress, the school you went to, the car you drive, the sports teams you support—all these affiliations are ways to tell both yourself and the world who you are and how to regard you. A great suit and the right tie and shirt and shoes that fit you great send the world a very specific signal about you.

Just like a great suit tells the world to treat you seriously, a great book tells the world the same.

Beyond that, a book can tell the world precisely how to regard you. Lots of different people wear suits, but only you will write your book, and it will be a unique record of your contribution to the world, so you get to decide what it means and how people will see you because of it.

You get to design the opinion others have of you through your book.

Robin Farmanfarmaian did this with her book, *The Patient as CEO*. As an attractive woman in the male-dominated world of Silicon Valley, Robin endured persistent sexism.

She had the knowledge and wisdom to be a leader in her own right, but what she realized was she needed to broadcast that wisdom so that her ideas—and not her gender—could precede her into the room.

Now things are very different.

> *"For me, the day my first book published, the sexual harassment stopped dead in its tracks. No man has touched me. No man has*

tried to talk me up to their hotel room. No man has asked me
to go get them coffee. No man has assumed I am the secretary.
My book changed the game overnight."

A Book Increases Your Visibility and Raises Your Profile

Whenever a media outlet wants to comment on something, they turn to the experts.

But how do they know someone is an expert? It's simple: they look for the people who wrote the book on that subject.

A book is the #1 signal of expertise.

Do you need more media coverage and visibility in your field? Write a book that establishes you as an expert, and media coverage will be 10x easier to get.

This is exactly what happened when entrepreneur Jonathan Siegel wrote his book, *The San Francisco Fallacy*, which detailed the fallacies of conventional wisdom in tech startups.

Once it was published, dozens of media outlets like *Inc.* and *Business Insider* reached out with requests. Siegel was already an expert in his field—he just needed a book to get media attention.

The same thing happened with Stephan Aarstol, CEO of

Tower Paddle Boards. He wrote a book about the innovative culture at his company, which allowed them to work 5-hour days. The media couldn't get enough of him and his book. Aarstol has been all over the media, with articles in *Inc., Forbes, Entrepreneur, Fast Company,* CNN, CNBC, Fox News, and others. Everyone in his world knows who he is.

I know this isn't surprising. How many times have you seen someone in your field get a ton of attention simply because they wrote a book?

Even if you know more than they do, they got the attention that you didn't.

And it's all because of their book.

A Book Establishes Your Authority and Credibility

Many people like to say that "a book is the new business card."

I disagree.

Everyone has a business card. You can go to Office Depot and get business cards. But you can't go to Office Depot and author a book.

Instead, I like to say that a book is the new college degree.

About 40 years ago, only 10–15% of people had college degrees. So if you had one, it was a major signal of credibility and authority. It meant something.

But now that nearly everyone goes to college (more than 70% of people), it doesn't set you apart. So what's a signal of credibility and authority now—one that's reliable and difficult, but uncommon?

A book.

A book shows you can commit to something and follow through. It shows you get things done.

And most importantly, it shows the world what you know. A book sets you up to be judged by your actual knowledge and work.

It's really easy to skirt by and still get a college degree. It's hard to manipulate your way into a good book.

Yes, being judged is risky. But that's why a book is a valid credential: it's a risk.

Most people aren't willing to take that risk. They're afraid of sharing their knowledge or showing the world what they know.

Robert Glazer, founder and CEO of Acceleration Partners,

took that risk with his book. He wrote about a difficult subject (performance marketing), which has a mixed reputation and a history of being a hotbed for the get-rich-quick schemes associated with affiliate marketers.

Glazer could have shied away from writing the book, but instead, he shared his knowledge in an open, vulnerable way.

Since publishing, he has increased his credibility and authority with both media and clients—and it was not only because of how good the book was but because of how honest it was and how many "secrets" he shared.

Basically, people trust him and find him credible because his book didn't shy away from the hard truths of his industry.

A book is also a credential for an entrepreneur like nothing else. It's proof of work, proof of contribution, proof that you did something that mattered to people.

Entrepreneurs don't get any other sort of credential—you get your company, and that's it. Which is really unfair, considering all the work you do. But you can have a book.

A book is proof of work, proof of contribution, proof that you did something that mattered to people, proof that you and your company made the world a better place. It's a credential that magnifies the impact of everything else you've ever done.

To be clear: you can't just spout nonsense, call it a book, and reap the benefits. To get credibility and authority from a book, you have to share valuable knowledge and ideas with your readers.

But if you can do that, you'll rocket past all your contemporaries who don't have a book, even if they're just as smart and accomplished as you are.

Suddenly, *you* will become the single go-to authority in your field.

Why?

Because people who write books on industries are the authorities in those industries. That's just how it works.

2. BUSINESS PAYOFFS

Books are one of the best ways to ensure that people know about you, think highly of you, and want to do business with you.

A Book Is the Perfect 24/7 Salesperson

The vast majority of successful entrepreneurs are great salespeople. They're usually not flashy, but they're convincing to others in face-to-face interactions.

The problem is that their ideas don't have any life beyond those moments when they're speaking.

That's when a book becomes invaluable.

Each book is a perfect salesperson. It presents all your sales tools in the exact manner you want them used.

When the book is finished, you've put your best ideas into one package. You've created something independent of yourself that 100% represents you and your work.

From the moment your book is published, it sells you and your ideas—24 hours a day, 365 days a year. Forever. *All around the world.*

When someone reads your book, they're introduced to you at your very best—no matter when or where they're reading it.

And not only does your book work 24/7, but it also works through as many copies as you have out in the world. It's an immediate 10x multiplier (at least) of your ideas. It's like putting 10,000 messages in a bottle. Somewhere it's going to come up on shore. Somebody's going to see that message.

Certified Financial Planner Mark Baird experienced this phenomenon with his book, *Rules to Riches: Eight Simple Strategies That Will Catapult You to Financial Security.*

Before he wrote the book, Mark did no public speaking. But after publishing the book, his credibility skyrocketed. He began averaging one speaking engagement a month with nothing but word-of-mouth referrals (not to mention, this has helped him double his assets under management).

He credits this referral chain directly to the book:

> *"You speak, you talk about the book, you sell a few copies, and they refer you to more people. It's a referral chain, and it's been very gratifying. I don't think it would have happened without the book."*

When entrepreneurs package their ideas in a book, it propels them beyond what they can do in a person-to-person sale. That's why book-creating entrepreneurs become national and global in their reach, impact, and results.

But here's the truth about 99.9% of all entrepreneurs in the world: they spend every day of their entire careers working to "sell their ideas" to their clientele and prospects.

It's really hard work that's getting harder. It's simply becoming continuously more difficult to get people's attention and money.

"Selling your ideas" is the worst way to be an entrepreneur.

A much easier and faster—not to mention more productive and profitable—way of creating your entrepreneurial future? Put all your problem-solving breakthroughs into a book, so your "ideas are selling you."

A book reverses that. A book is an "idea selling you." In the 21st century, having your "ideas selling you" will enable you to multiply your entrepreneurial capabilities, resources, opportunities, and success in ways that have never before been possible.

Your ideas are always working on your behalf. They're always making new connections, always opening doors, always creating new opportunities.

It's absolutely the best way of being an entrepreneur.

A Book Reduces Your Risk to Others and Creates Word of Mouth

A book makes people more comfortable working with you, taking a risk on you, and introducing you to others.

In other words, they might say, "Well, I'm going to bring this guy in. He's an author. If nothing else, just read his book."

The mere fact that you've gone through the experience of writing a book and producing it in a professional way is a vetting process in itself. A thought has been vetted and tested and presented to the world. Your work can be checked. And that vetting and checking is a credential.

This credentialing that books do also facilitates the best marketing there is: word of mouth.

When someone you trust tells you to use something, you listen. That's why the best marketing tool is anything that helps other people talk about you and your business.

A book enables word of mouth better than almost any other marketing.

If you write a book that's valuable to a group of people, they'll want to talk about it at cocktail parties with others who could also benefit from it.

Why? *Because it makes them look better.* That's how word of mouth works.

There are many examples of professionals benefiting from the word-of-mouth marketing their books provided.

Entrepreneur Melissa Gonzalez's book, *The Pop Up Paradigm*, created a top-line sales gain of 33%, year over year. She estimates that 75% of her clients know about her book before they hire her, and over 30% have read it.

Because of this, Melissa has reversed her sales process. Now clients come in wanting to pitch Melissa to get her to work with them—like I said earlier, she went from the buyer to the seller.

A Book Gets You New Clients and Opportunities

The #1 search engine is Google. YouTube is #2. Know what #3 is?

Amazon.

More importantly, it's the #1 search engine for professionals (ranking even higher than LinkedIn, which surprises me, but is true). When people look for a credible expert or authority, they want the person who literally "wrote the book" on the topic.

Having a great book lets people know exactly who you are and how you can help them. It brings searchers right to you.

It's the best marketing tool you can use—not only to build your brand but to actually attract clients.

Here's a great example of how this works:

When we started Scribe, we got a lot of early traction. I quickly realized we had a rocket ship we didn't know how to fly. So what did I do? I went to Amazon to find books on how to scale a company.

As it turns out, there aren't a lot of great books out there about managing and scaling a fast-growing company. The best I could find was written by Cameron Herold (it's called *Double Double*). The title isn't great, but the book itself is amazing.

I read it and thought, *This is genius, but I need more. I need this guy to coach me directly.*

I reached out to Cameron, and he became my executive coach, then got a piece of the company. That's how valuable he's been.

There are probably 500 other people out there who could have taught me the same things, but Cameron was the only one who had a great book. His book gave me proof of his knowledge, and it convinced me that he was the one who should teach me.

It was the best possible sales pitch—because it showed me he knew his stuff.

A Book Attracts Talent That Levels Up Whole Companies

A book is a talent-attractor.

The best way to find like-minded people is to talk about what you're doing and why. And a book is the best way to do that.

It establishes what you believe in, what purpose and mission your company serves, and why it matters to the world.

You begin attracting people who can sense that a big game is being played. They sense that their talents will be appreciated and utilized and that they'll be able to do great work.

Mark Organ's book, *The Messenger Is the Message,* is a perfect example. His book spells out the beliefs of his company, Influitive, and its employees. It has resonated with people on such a deep level that they now use it as a tool to attract and retain top-tier talent. He estimates that he's hired almost a dozen top-tier people as a direct result of the book.

Not only does it unify your current team, but it can bring new people into your company or organization.

Dan Sullivan's podcast manager is another great example. He was in radio for about 20 years before he joined their team. And he told Dan:

"It's the content and context of your podcasts that cinched me

on the job. You know, I've heard that you were a good company and that you had done all of this, but the ideas you're expressing are in the world, and once I saw them, I knew I had to be part of this."

When you start getting your talent (both customers and internal team members) on the idea, context, and purpose level, that's when you see the real payoff.

But you can't do that in person all the time. So how are you going to do it?

With a book.

3. IMPACT ON OTHERS PAYOFFS

Books are one of the best ways to leave a lasting and valuable impact on other people.

Books Help People

Authors often tell me, "I just want my book to help people."

It's an admirable goal, and it's definitely achievable. In fact, if you want your book to do well, it *should* help other people.

But when pressed, most authors don't have any idea how their book will actually help.

It's not that the book *can't* help. It's just that they don't know specifically *how* it will.

The answer is actually quite simple:

A book helps people by giving them the information, skills, motivation, or perspective to change something in their life for the better.

In short: a book creates a desired transformation in them.

In fact, the most successful authors are the ones who are able to help a specific audience overcome a specific problem (or provide them with a unique benefit).

By simply writing your book, you'll help relieve someone's suffering of that problem and transform their life forever.

That's the difference you'll make.

One of my favorite examples of this is Jeb White's book, *Breaking Into College.* Even though it added 6 figures in direct sales to his business, what Jeb was most excited about is how disadvantaged kids used his book to get into the colleges of their dreams.

He shows kids who otherwise can't even imagine going to college exactly how they can do it, step by step. They go from not thinking this is an option, to thinking it might be an option, to realizing they can do it, to then actually doing it. Entire families are changed forever.

All from a book.

Books Scale Your Impact

Many authors want to make an impact on people, but what they don't realize is that their book can scale the impact they already have.

What does it mean to scale your impact?

It's similar to scaling a company (i.e., making it bigger). Consider your life now: you might be helping a lot of people, but chances are you know them already. They're typically connected to you or your direct community in some way.

But what would happen if you could help people you don't even know? Or people you'll never meet?

That's the power of a book.

Yes, you can help many people in your regular life, but a book scales your impact and helps you reach more people in a more profound way. It allows people to find you and get your help *without* you having to spend any time with them.

Think about it: if you can help hundreds of people in your business, you can help thousands through your book.

A great example is Nic Kusmich. Nic owns one of the best Facebook ad agencies in the world. He's directly helped hundreds of businesses grow and scale.

But his services and seminars are expensive. One of the reasons he wrote his book, *Give*, was to help people who couldn't afford him.

And one day that paid off, when a 17-year-old waiter used his book to start his own business:

> *"Mr. Kusmich, I wanted to write to you and tell you how much your book meant to me. I can't thank you enough for the knowledge in your book. It was amazing and became my bible for my new career. It helped me start my own Facebook business, and I'd never be able to do that without you."*

Nic is now helping people he's never met, in places he's never gone.

That's what a book can help you do: expand your reach and scale your impact.

Books Improve Family Relationships

Books can also transform relationships and connect families.

How?

By helping the people in your life understand what you do and why it's important.

This is a common byproduct of publishing a book, but it's one that often takes authors by surprise. That's because most of their loved ones don't understand what they do on a day-to-day basis. It's not their fault. We just live in a world where most business professionals have very complicated jobs that are difficult for the outside world to comprehend.

But a book helps families understand your work. It connects what you do with their reality. It shows them the impact you have on the world and why your work matters.

Reading your book is a profoundly inspiring and transformative experience for the people you care most about.

Sam Marella's book, *Your Retirement Game Plan*, is a great example. As a financial advisor, Sam has received an influx of new clients and made a lot of money from his book.

But what does he value most about his book? That it helped his daughter see him differently.

"I was totally outside my comfort zone writing a book, so feeling the weight of it in my hand and seeing my name on the cover was an aha moment for me. As for my daughter's admiration? Well, that was just icing on the cake."

4. PERSONAL GROWTH PAYOFFS

Books help you grow as a person in a way nothing else can.

Books Give You Confidence and Pride of Accomplishment

Writing a book is difficult. That's why most people don't do it.

No matter how easy writing is for you (I'm a professional writer and it's hard for me), completing a book is still a difficult process. It requires a lot of courage to start a book and see it through.

To write a book, you have to believe your ideas are valid and worth sharing.

You have to challenge and overcome anything that stands in the way of your self-worth.

It forces you to confront difficult emotional issues and challenge your fears, whether it's the fear of failure, the fear of being judged, or even the fear of success. It might even force you to address things you haven't thought about *for years*.

These were exact thoughts of Kirk Drake, author of *CU 2.0: A Guide for Credit Unions Competing in the Digital Age*. He wanted to help save the credit union industry but was afraid his book wouldn't measure up.

> *"What makes me think I have something important to say? Can I actually make a difference? If I was going to write a book, I'd have to put 100% of my heart and soul into it. I just didn't know if my 100% would be good enough."*

But once you've confronted those fears, it becomes a source of immense confidence and pride. It's proof that you've achieved something hard and worthwhile.

In fact, despite his fears, Kirk's book went on to be an immense success. His book has become legendary in the credit union world, led to millions in revenue, and doubled the size of his firm.

And not only did that give him confidence—he says that he's most proud of the transformations he's seen in credit unions as a result of his book. He has hundreds of case studies about the impact his book has made on his industry.

Writing your book means you've done something in your life that matters—not just to you but to other people.

It's a valuable accomplishment to mark off your bucket list.

And better yet, it's an achievement that can never be taken away.

You can think of it as comparable to your wardrobe. Harry Rosen, one of the greatest tailors in Canada's upper men's affluent market, once told Dan Sullivan,

> *"It's not style that you want. It's style confidence that you want. Style confidence is when you have a style that makes you so confident, you can go to any public gathering where people are well-dressed and be the only person not worried about how you're dressed."*

There's a "book confidence" you can acquire as well.

When you're in a room where other people have ideas, but *you're* the idea person who's got a book—that gives you confidence, both in your idea and in your position in the room, because you know you've done something hard that means you belong.

Books Give You Creative Expression

A book, by its very definition, is a creative expression.

Not only will writing a book improve your creativity—it also signals to others that you're a creative person with original ideas. Writing a book is one of the best ways to explore your creativity and express yourself more authentically.

A book is the most uniquely designed school system that you'll ever be in. It lets you focus on your unique ability and show the world who you are in a way that makes you look best.

In other words, it's where you're the professor, the course teacher, and the student. It's the most complete self-education experience that anyone can have. You only chose the topic because it's of central interest to you. And the evidence that you use as proof that the course is worth taking comes from your own experience.

This was the case for Janet Newman, who wrote her book, *Living in the Chemical Age*, about the prevalence of toxins and harmful chemicals in our environment, food, and everyday products. Not only has she helped her readers live healthier lives—she has discovered her own voice and creative expression in the process.

> *"I found my voice. That's really the easiest way to describe it. The book has helped me to really express myself and feel like what I have to say is not only important but that people want to hear it. And so that's kind of a new muscle for me. It's something I had to get used to. If I had to wrap it up and put a little pretty bow on it, I'd say I found my voice."*

Books Create Self-Improvement and Skill Development

Writing a book will, by its very nature, force you to get better at many things. You'll become a better writer, a better editor, and a better storyteller.

But more importantly, you'll also understand your ideas better.

That's not to say you don't already have the knowledge necessary to write your book. Most professionals I've worked with are well-versed in their fields, and they're experts in their industries.

They just don't always know how to explain their work or ideas to other people.

Writing a book changes that.

It forces you to be articulate—not only about what you do but about how you communicate it to others effectively.

Effective communication is an invaluable skill, and it's a necessary part of writing a book. By the time you finish, you'll be an expert at it.

Marketing expert Will Leach did exactly this with his book, *Marketing to Mindstates*. He realized there was a ton of great stuff he was using with his company, but nobody had translated it into something that was usable—so he took on the challenge.

As Will describes it, writing a book was both rewarding and humbling. He had to challenge his ideas, dig deeper into his stories and concepts, and translate those ideas into something usable for a wide audience.

> *"Writing a book was both the hardest and most fun thing I've ever done. And I was shocked by the way it impacted the rest of my life. I thought I was a good writer and thinker already, and maybe I was, but writing a book made me way better at both. I even understood my own ideas better than before."*

No matter how well you know what you do, explaining it to others always helps you know it better. That is the point of the saying, "When one teaches, two learn."

Going through the process of making the implicit into the explicit teaches you what you know and how to explain. You get better, and you get better at what you already know how to do.

Books Help You Escape from Your Ideas

One of the greatest things about publishing a book is that you get to escape from your old thoughts. Once you put those thoughts into a book, your mind is cleared.

That's why people who spend 25 or 30 years with a book idea are literally prisoners.

Let's say someone wants to write an autobiographical book. They eventually become a prisoner of their experiences. They're unhappy because they want to put those experiences into a book for others to read.

But they never do that. So they're eternally frustrated.

Then there are those people who have a technique, method, or perspective they want to write about. After a while, their idea becomes static. It's like cement in their mind.

They sit with this thought constantly, and they can't get free of it because it hasn't been released into the world.

Take entrepreneur Matt Bertulli, for example. He is a master at integrating technology with commerce and started a business, Demac Media, dedicated to helping merchants scale their business. He sat with his ideas for 2 years before he fully committed to writing his book, *Anything, Anywhere.*

> *"I thought a book could help me show people how to create better stuff and reach customers in a low-friction way. I had no business plan for the book—I just wanted to get it out of my head and into the world."*

Until you fully commit to writing your book, you're trapped by these experiences and ideas.

That's why the first book is always the most difficult book. There are a lot of emotions and thoughts tied up in it. But once it's finished, your mind is free.

Dan talks about this all the time—until he started writing books, he would be stuck with his ideas. But now he puts them into the world, and they are gone from his mind, and he's free to think about the next thing.

The same is true for me. I can tell you as someone who wrote 4 autobiographical books, writing essentially frees me from the stories and thoughts in them. It's like once I commit them to paper and put them out into the world, they are no longer mine to carry.

It's the strangest thing, but it's true. I can't tell you how many times people have come up to me and told me about loving some story of mine in one of my books, and of course I remember the event and the story, but I feel as though it's from a different life.

Books Show Intentionality

Books show effectiveness and intentionality.

Intentionality is the ability to lock on a desirable future result. It's the great human skill. Entrepreneurs have it more than the general population, and it's a very rare capability in the world.

With intentionality, we can take a new situation and create an entirely new purpose with that situation. We can pull in new kinds of information. We can create an actionable, measurable result, and we can achieve it.

Books are one of the best ways to bring you back to intentionality. When you're writing a book, you'll hit on a lot of different dimensions—but you can't include everything in one book.

You have to decide:

What's the actual point of this book? What's the result I want?

There's a power in that. It enables you to effectively create something that's going to actually achieve the result you want.

And you don't even have to be there in person to create that result. When you write a book, you invest so much of it with who you really are, what you really believe, and what you think is really possible. Simply reading it will have the same impact on someone as if they met you at your best in person (we already talked about that in the business section as well).

Functional nutritionist Dr. Robert Silverman is a prime example. He decided exactly what result he wanted from his book, which allowed him to create something that would achieve that result.

> "I didn't want to write a book to get on Dr. Oz or CNBC. I wanted to write a book to exponentially increase the presence of my voice in the marketplace. I wanted to get my knowledge out in a way that allowed people to learn from me even if I wasn't in the room."

Silverman wrote and edited a book that was specifically designed to impart his unique knowledge of functional nutrition to the world. As a result, the book has since become a permanent teaching tool and has helped people he's never even met.

> "The ripples of my knowledge are now spreading beyond my private practice and the walls of a single auditorium. I'm always looking for long-term solutions for my patients. This book is my long-term solution to functional nutrition."

5. LEGACY PAYOFFS

A book ensures that you leave something behind for others.

A Book Helps You Leave a Legacy

How do you leave a legacy?

You leave a legacy by doing things that make other people's lives better.

There are many ways to make other people's lives better—and a book is one of the best means of doing it.

This is because—as mentioned earlier—a book is written to help other people. If you write it with your audience in mind, and you understand the transformation they seek, then it's inevitable that your book will help people.

It's also a way to ensure that your mission and your legacy survive long after you're gone. There's nothing wrong with only helping people in your immediate sphere of influence, but that help stops when you die.

A legacy left in a book can carry on for generations after you're gone.

For example, we're all influenced by the legacies of Socrates or Anne Frank or Malcolm X simply because they put their knowledge into a book.

A lot of people do important work, but not a lot of people write books about it. Writing a book means that other people will look up to you, respect you, and admire you.

You'll have made the world better, and you can be proud of that—and that is a legacy.

Author Shannon Miles experienced this firsthand with her book, *The Third Option.*

After becoming pregnant with her first child, Shannon was forced to make the choice between working full-time or not at all. This experience inspired her to create BELAY Inc., a virtual staffing company built on the idea that people should have more than 2 choices when it comes to work.

Shannon wrote her book to chronicle this journey. She knew her story could inspire others who were ready to make a change—and it has. Thousands of people have shared their triumphs with Shannon. And one woman, in particular, was especially impacted by her story:

> *"She told me she was raised by a stay-at-home mom, so she thought when she was ready to have kids, she'd have to leave her job. She felt trapped. After reading the book, she saw there*

was another way. That tells me, even for people who aren't ready to make a decision, the book is planting seeds for their future."

A Book Provides Future Intellectual Capital

A book is a dimension of you. It's a way to provide your team and the future leaders of your company with additional resources should you no longer be around.

Dan Sullivan considers this with every quarterly book he releases.

He's produced 20 books in the last 5 years, and each one serves the purpose of setting up the next quarter's workshops.

The book is built in as a useful component of the main activity: the workshops. It supports the coaches because it's his ideas, not the coaches' ideas. The book prepares them.

It's also future intellectual capital if (god forbid) anything happens to Dan. Every book has 10 or 20 concepts that his team could take and turn into a program.

It's like an emergency fire extinguisher box hanging on a wall. In case of emergency, your team can break the glass and read the manual.

Books ensure that your ideas last forever. The more you

write, the more ideas you leave behind, and the more your team can build upon.

Take a look at Apple. It's pretty easy to see that there isn't any more Steve Jobs left on the shelf. You knew when they ran out of stuff that Steve had developed. The products were bloated, confusing, and hard to use. Don't do that to your team.

A Book Is Proof of Impact and Existence

I believe the greatest cause of mental illness is twofold.

One is the idea that what you experience, what you think about, and what you feel has no reality in the world.

The other is the idea that who you are and what you passionately believe in has no impact on other people. In other words, that your existence is just passing through. That you don't even leave a shadow on a sunny day.

The bigger the population gets, and the more connected we are to different forms of media, the harder it is for individuals to have a confident sense of self in the world.

It's the biggest question people face: *Am I real? Am I uniquely, individually real?*

They don't think: *I can see there are a lot of things that look like me wandering about.*

That's why illegal drugs are so prevalent and why psychiatrists are such a big deal. A lot of people just don't have proof of existence.

But a book is proof that you exist.

When you have a book, there's something of you that's out there operating in the world. And whether people like it or dislike it, or like you or dislike you, doesn't matter. They're responding to you.

Those people will take action. They'll come back to you and say, "That book of yours—that's made a real difference in my life."

It's proof of impact and proof of reality.

Lorenzo Gomez's book, *The Cilantro Diaries*, is a great example of this. Gomez did not realize it when he began writing, but there were virtually no Hispanic CEOs who wrote books, and none who wrote them in an engaging way that resonated with younger kids from working-class families.

But his unique perspective resonated deeply with his community. His book directly impacted inner-city Hispanic kids, who came from the same poor neighborhoods that he did. That connection, created by Gomez's book, became an irrefutable proof of impact and existence.

As a result, Lorenzo has spoken to thousands of young kids, especially Hispanic kids from the neighborhoods he grew up in, and he even did the keynote at the graduation ceremony for the University of Texas, San Antonio—even though he didn't even go to college.

So much of early entrepreneurship is difficult. You have to supply your own batteries. You can't plug into the grid like a lot of people can.

Having more and more outside proof of impact establishes your reality. Because, to a certain extent, we're inside of ourselves. We have millions of experiences that nobody else is ever going to know about.

But the key is, how do you establish irrefutable proof in the world that what you're feeling and thinking inside actually has existence and an impact outside of yourself?

I think books are a great way to do it.

SUMMARY

To summarize, this is everything you get from writing a book:

1. PRESTIGE/BRAND PAYOFFS

Your book establishes your authority and raises your prestige in many ways:

1. Levels up your identity (you're an author)
2. Positions you in the world
3. Increases your visibility and raises your profile
4. Establishes your authority and credibility

2. BUSINESS PAYOFFS

Your book helps your business in many ways:

1. Is the perfect 24/7 salesperson
2. Reduces your risk to others and facilitates word of mouth
3. Gets you new clients and opportunities
4. Recruits top-tier talent for your business

3. IMPACT ON OTHERS PAYOFFS

Your book impacts others in many ways:

1. Helps people

2. Scales your impact
3. Improves your family relationships

4. PERSONAL GROWTH PAYOFFS

Your book helps you grow as a person in many ways:

1. Gives you confidence and pride of accomplishment
2. Gives you creative expression
3. Creates self-improvement and skill development
4. Helps you escape from your idea
5. Shows intentionality

5. LEGACY PAYOFFS

Your book helps you leave something behind for others in many ways:

1. Helps you leave a legacy
2. Provides future intellectual capital
3. Is proof of impact and existence

PART 2

SELL YOURSELF BEFORE YOU START

A lot of authors start writing a book without being sold on it. That's one of the biggest mistakes you can make. Dan Sullivan says:

> *"Ten years ago, I had the biggest breakthrough of my life. I discovered that all the difficulties, frustrations, failures, and setbacks in my personal and entrepreneurial life came from a single cause:*
>
> ***Attempting to do anything, in any situation, without first selling myself on the reason and results of the activity or project."***

That's why the first thing you have to do with a book is sell yourself on it.

You have to see the desirable end result—that you are, down the road, a better person because you wrote this book. You have to give yourself the maximum self-reward at the end. Dan does this with every project (and now I do, too, thanks to being in the Strategic Coach program).

So now that you know all the reasons that can make books such a powerful unfair advantage for entrepreneurs, it's time to sell yourself on writing your book...or not.

In this section, I'll guide you through 8 questions that will either sell you on writing your book—or help you see you're not ready, and you can give it up.

STEP 1: SELL YOURSELF ON WRITING A BOOK
WHY DO YOU WANT TO WRITE A BOOK?

It's simple: A weak purpose equals a bad book. A great purpose equals a great book.

To write a great book, you must be really clear about the difference you want it to make. The difference you want it to make for you, and most importantly, the difference that you want it to make for other people.

There are 2 ways to answer this question, and for the best results, you should address both.

*1. The Bean Counter Answer: What exactly will you get
from writing a book?*

Imagine it's 2 years after your book was published, and we're looking back on the results together. What has the book done for you that made the effort worthwhile? What's your ideal outcome?

In this case, I consider the ideal outcome from a more practical perspective. It's what you'd put on a spreadsheet to give to the "bean counters."

It could be that you're going to sell 500 copies by New Year's, or get 5 new clients by October, or speak at a big conference, or any combination of things like that.

Whatever the ideal outcome is for you, make sure it's a specific, measurable, achievable, and realistic accomplishment.

*2. The Deeper Answer: What's the real reason writing a
book appeals to you?*

Sometimes your motivations for writing a book can't be easily measured. And that's completely fine.

*Money and numbers are **not** the only ways to measure a book's
impact.*

Even though the branding and business payoffs of a book

are great economically, I honestly believe the emotional or intangible reasons for writing a book matter most to authors in the long run.

That's because books can improve lives in ways that simply can't be measured just in money or things that show up on spreadsheets.

Perhaps you want to help others transform their lives or to improve your relationships.

Or maybe you want to scale your impact and leave a lasting legacy.

What if you just want to prove that you were here and that your work mattered?

Those are okay. As you learned in part 1, they are excellent reasons to write a book—often the BEST reasons.

There's no easy way to quantify these goals, but as long as you're clear about your purpose and the difference your book will make in your readers' lives, you'll be on your way to a great book.

STEP 2: FIGURE OUT WHO WILL CARE

3. WHO'S THE IDEAL READER FOR YOUR BOOK?

In essence, *who do you want to be a hero to?*

If you want your book to be successful and reach the objectives you set out for it, you need an audience—and you need to figure out who that audience is *before* you start writing.

The audience is a single group of people who share the specific problem your book solves.

Notice I said "single." It's very hard to write a book with wide appeal. There's literally no book in the world intended for everyone—and your book isn't the exception.

But that's a good thing. Attracting a wide audience doesn't benefit you. The key to writing a book that helps you in business is narrowing your audience down to only the people your book is intended to help—the people you can be a hero to.

An easy way to understand who those people are is by thinking about who you've helped in the past. Ask yourself the same questions Dan asks his entrepreneurs:

> *"When in the past have you been a hero to other people? When did they really value what you did? And when did that make you feel really proud?"*

It's hard to be confident about your future until you feel more confident about your past. This applies to books as well.

The more you envision a real person you can help, the more excited and confident you will be about writing this book for them.

4. WHY WILL THEY CARE?

If your perfect reader reads and implements the ideas in your book, how will their life change for the better? How does your book help them solve a problem or create a transformation in their life?

In short, *why will the reader care about your book?*

The harsh but true reality is that your audience doesn't care about your book. They only care about what your book gets them.

Think about it: do you ever decide to buy a book because of the author's goals for writing that book?

Of course not. You only buy a book if you believe the book will help *you.*

If you aren't sure why your book matters to your reader, chances are you've made your book only about you, and you haven't spent any time thinking about who would read it and why.

Don't beat yourself up; this is a common mistake that many authors make.

Instead, get back to the roots of why this book will make a difference in your readers' lives. Ask yourself:

Why will the reader care? How can your knowledge help someone solve a problem or create a transformation in their life?

STEP 3: FIND THE OBSTACLES AND FLIP THEM

5. WHY HAVEN'T YOU WRITTEN YOUR BOOK YET?

Writing a book can be a challenging and intimidating endeavor. As such, there are countless excuses people use to delay their book.

There are lots of reasons: not enough time is a common one. Or not the right resources. Or not knowing how to do it.

But if you're like most authors, the real reason you haven't started your book is that you're afraid.

Maybe you're afraid that you don't have a book in you or that your idea isn't original enough. Or perhaps you're afraid your book won't be good and that no one will care about it—or worse, that it will upset people.

Or maybe you're just afraid that your book will make you look stupid.

Whatever your fears are, you're not alone. All authors start in the same position: riddled with anxiety, uncertainty, and fear.

I've been writing professionally for nearly 2 decades, and I still deal with these fears in every book I write. It's perfectly normal.

But once you figure out what fear is holding you back, then you can come up with a plan to deal with and ultimately overcome it.

6. WHAT'S YOUR PLAN?

How will you overcome these obstacles and challenges?

It's completely okay to be afraid and nervous to start your book. But it's not okay to let those fears stand in the way of accomplishing your goal.

You need to have a plan to overcome them and get started.

But if you don't have a plan yet or don't know where to start, it's fine. That's what the rest of this book is about.

STEP 4: CLOSING THE SALE

7. WORST RESULT?

What if you don't write your book? What happens to you (and your readers)?

Consider your readers first. Imagine the person you'll be helping with your book. Think of them very specifically. Imagine the pain they're in now. *Feel* the suffering they have because they haven't read your book.

Think about how much they need your knowledge, and what's going to happen to their lives if they don't get it.

Then, think about yourself.

What benefits are you missing out on by not writing your book? How will your business suffer or plateau without the advantages a book provides?

If thinking about what will happen if you don't write your book scares you, *good*. That's the point.

Nothing new, better, or different happens in the world unless a particular formula is at work:

Fear x Excitement = Transformation

The first element of any kind of significant individual or organizational improvement—in any area of activity—comes from "scaring" people into making a decision and taking action that creates better performance and results.

That's what fear is all about: if you don't change the way you're thinking and acting, right now, you're going to get hammered by the world in ways that you'll really regret.

Fear of a much worse future is the single biggest reason why people change their "KASH," which stands for Knowledge, Attitude, Skills, and Habits. All personal progress in the world, in every area of activity, comes from transforming KASH.

"Knowledge" means that they have to look at things in a different way, using new evidence and principles. "Attitude" means that they have to change how they feel about the world so that their heart is in alignment with their head. "Skills" means that they have to change how they think and feel into new ways of getting successful results. And "Habits" means that their new way of achieving superior results has to become automatic.

So in this book, I am trying to scare you into a significant decision and into a different kind of action.

I'm trying to do everything I can to convince you that if you don't significantly improve your creative ability to package and distribute your best problem-solving innovations to a much larger audience, you're going to get hammered by the commoditizing forces of global change.

In short, if you don't write your book, you're going to suffer (and so will your reader).

8. BEST RESULT?

What if you do write your book? What happens to you (and your readers)?

Think back to the unique payoffs outlined in part 1. Consider all the advantages that you'll receive once your book is complete.

How will having a book transform your life?

For one, it will elevate your brand. A book levels up your identity, positions you in the world, raises your profile, and establishes your authority.

It will also ensure that people know about you, think highly of you, and want to do business with you. Your book will sell you directly to your readers, generating leads and bringing in new clients.

It will even help you grow as a person, providing a sense of confidence and creative accomplishment.

But how will your book transform your readers' lives?

Your book will give people the information they need to change something in their life for the better. And it will allow you to spread your impact to thousands of people.

The world will be a better place because of you.

By writing your book, you'll leave a lasting legacy.

I could go on and on, but really think about what you will get, and what you will value from that.

READY TO START?

If you're totally sold and want to start outlining your book, move on to part 3.

But if you feel like there are other objections still lurking in your mind, keep reading and we'll help you address them.

ANSWERING THE OBJECTIONS

For most entrepreneurs—probably 97%—the idea of writing a book immediately undermines their confidence.

Why?

Because they don't see themselves as "authors."

I've been writing for nearly 2 decades, and I'd honestly forgotten about this until recently. When I spoke to Dan about this fear, he said:

> *"This is the biggest obstacle. This is the thing we must address. And I get it. I've dealt with this obstacle myself. Once I overcame it, my ability to package my ideas in the form of books, essays, articles, and blogs went through the roof. And it's a big part of what made Strategic Coach successful. But yeah, this fear of not being a 'real author' crippled me for years."*

In order to quickly produce a powerful Big Book Payoff, you have to forget all your conventional and demoralizing notions of what it means to be an "author."

We're not going to ask you to "open a vein and bleed" on your keyboard.

We're not going to tell you to learn a bunch of stuff that reminds you of school.

We'll never advocate spending a bunch of time doing something that's not in your unique capability (though we will tell you to expand your capabilities a bit).

The only goal of this entire project is to increase a unique entrepreneurial capability—the capability to have "your ideas sell you" throughout the world.

Your book will give you an unfair advantage. It will set you apart from everyone else who doesn't have this capability.

In fact, 99.9% of entrepreneurs who think about writing a book never do. That's because they don't know how to easily determine the most important message they need to communicate to their clientele and prospects.

In short, they think they have to become a professional writer and do everything the hard way.

As we've discussed, you don't have to do that. Here are the ways to avoid this issue (and all the fears around it):

1. WRITE ONLY ABOUT WHAT FASCINATES AND MOTIVATES YOU.

There are a lot of boring books in the world. They were written by people who weren't excited about their subject, didn't really like their readers, and weren't clear on why they were writing.

In the Strategic Coach program, Dan teaches that the number-one reason to write a book is to communicate the most important "Unique Ability" activity that you do as an entrepreneur—in other words, the single activity that will keep you fascinated and motivated for the rest of your life.

In his program, they coach you to stay inside of your Unique Ability. The same idea applies to writing your book.

Always think and communicate from a permanently deepening and expanding framework of experience, where:

1. You have a lifetime passion.
2. You can be a hero to the clientele that you most want to help.
3. Being a passionate hero increasingly multiplies your finances and marketplace reputation.

2. WRITE ONLY TO THOSE YOU NEED AND THOSE WHO CAN USE YOUR HELP.

If you take all the different "knowledge products" that Dan has written over the past 25 years, the total output would add up to 80 books of 80 pages.

Every one of these books—including this one—has been written exclusively for entrepreneurs who can benefit from using Strategic Coach concepts and tools (and, of course, who would be interested in participating in the program).

As a result of Dan's writing, thousands of entrepreneurs have signed up for Strategic Coach. He has been invited to speak at hundreds of marketing events, has been interviewed hundreds of times, and has been asked to write hundreds of articles.

When he writes, he does it to support bigger Strategic Coach paydays.

That strategy can be your strategy. If you had set out in life to be a famous author, you would've made different choices and taken a different path. But you didn't.

Instead, you chose to be a uniquely creative problem-solver in a specific market niche of the rapidly expanding global economy. And that's where you'll be growing, achieving, and succeeding for the rest of your entrepreneurial career.

The *Big Book Payoff* will enable you to take the value you've already created and multiply it many times over—by focusing your book on who you already help, and who you can help in the future.

3. WRITE ONLY ABOUT SOMETHING YOU'VE ALREADY BEEN PAID FOR.

When I pick up any nonfiction book, it only takes me about a minute to determine whether the author actually gets paid for practicing what he or she is preaching (or gets paid for actually delivering the value that they're proposing).

Both Dan and I teach the same thing: never ever write about something unless you have a proven track record of success, as defined by getting paid by satisfied clients and customers.

By doing this, you will ensure that you are confident about it—because you've done it—and you can know you'll be helping people.

4. GIVE A RECIPE FOR SUCCESSFUL CHANGE.

There are 2 kinds of books I hate reading:

1. Those that describe problems but don't offer practical solutions.
2. Those that promise a big breakthrough but don't explain the practical steps to achieve it.

That's why Dan always tells his readers how they can get to solutions and breakthroughs. He lays out detailed "recipes" for them to follow to create successful change.

Same with me. In my book *The Scribe Method*, I lay out our entire book writing process, start to finish. And we put the whole training up for free on ScribeBookSchool.com as well.

It's literally EVERY piece of information you need to write a book.

Even if they never meet me or pay me a cent for my services, I want them to get maximum, future-changing value from everything I write.

This is how we recommend all entrepreneurs write their books: with a specific and detailed recipe for change or transformation.

5. SPEND MONEY TO MAKE TIME.

Time is one of the biggest obstacles entrepreneurs face when writing a book.

Not only do they have to set aside the actual quantity of time needed to write a book, but they also need the discipline required to do it. Dan Sullivan likes to tell his entrepreneurs:

"You don't have to be the writer. But you have to be the author."

There are tons of ways people will write your book for you, but you have to have an idea that's yours.

The words "author" and "authority" are closely related. They both convey the sense of originator, creator, or expert.

In this world, it's much more difficult to come up with original solutions and breakthroughs than it is to be someone who's good at putting words together.

As an entrepreneur, you've probably spent years or decades creating unique solutions in the marketplace. All that problem-solving has made you a creative, authoritative thinker and expert. If you've done that, you have everything that is the key to being a successful author.

There are many famous authors who didn't actually write their influential bestsellers. If you feel you can't—or just don't want to—write your book, it's easy to find someone else to do it for you, and I will walk you through exactly how to do that later in the book.

What matters here is not whether your hands are on the keyboard typing. That is not what makes an author.

The ideas are what make an author. If the ideas and the experience are yours, then finding a way to translate that into a book is simple.

SUMMARY

To summarize, this is how to sell yourself on writing a book (or not):

STEP 1: SELL YOURSELF ON WRITING A BOOK

Ask yourself: *Why do you want to write your book?* There are 2 ways to answer this question:

1. The Bean Counter Answer: What exactly will you get from writing a book?

This is usually the quantifiable stuff, what to tell your CFO to convince them to let you spend the money to write this book—things like money, prestige, business, visibility, etc.

2. The Deeper Answer: What's the real reason writing a book appeals to you?

This is usually the harder-to-measure stuff, but stuff that matters a lot—things like legacy, personal growth, relationships, impact, and purpose.

STEP 2: FIGURE OUT WHO WILL CARE

3. Who's the ideal reader of your book?

This is about who your book is written for. In essence, *who do you want to be a hero to?*

4. Why will they care?

Now you have to understand why they're going to care about

your book. *How can your knowledge help someone solve a problem or create a transformation in their life?*

STEP 3: FIND THE OBSTACLES AND FLIP THEM

5. Why haven't you written your book yet?

This is about understanding what has held you back in the past, so you can ensure that you avoid or solve that problem this time and get your book done.

6. What's your plan?

How will you overcome these obstacles and challenges?

STEP 4: CLOSING THE SALE

7. Worst Result?

What if you don't write your book? What happens to you (and your readers)?

8. Best Result?

What if you do write your book? What happens to you (and your readers)?

ANSWERING THE OBJECTIONS

For most entrepreneurs—probably 97%—the idea of writing a book immediately undermines their confidence. So how do you solve it?

1. Write only about what fascinates and motivates you.
2. Write only to those you need and those who can use your help.
3. Write only about something you've already been paid for.
4. Give a recipe for successful change.
5. Spend money to make time.

PART 3

THE ENTREPRENEUR BOOK SPECIFIC OUTLINE PROCESS

By now, you should know exactly what you get from writing a book, and what your reasons are for writing it. This ensures that you're sold on writing your book.

You should also know who the ideal reader is and why they'll care. This ensures that there will be an audience for the book (which is how you get what you want).

You should know what's stopped you from writing your book in the past, and you might know your plan to overcome those issues (if you don't, that's okay—we explain the plan in the following instructions in this book).

Lastly, you should know the worst thing that will happen

if you don't write this book—and the best thing that will happen if you do.

What you *don't* know yet is how to put all of this together.

I've been helping entrepreneurs write and publish books for nearly a decade. In my experience, if a busy entrepreneur doesn't quickly establish a clear and confident structure for their book, they stop and don't come back.

That's why I've designed this chapter to take you only 60 minutes of total work: 30 minutes of reading and 30 minutes of outlining.

If you spend the next hour on this, you can permanently change how you communicate your most valuable solutions and ideas to the world.

THE 30-MINUTE BOOK OUTLINE

This outline process is specific to entrepreneurs, and I'm going to tell you something very different than how we teach other people:

Don't spend too much time outlining.

30 minutes is more than enough. All you need to do is get your basic ideas down, and in a structure that makes sense.

They don't have to be perfect, and in fact, if they are perfect, it means you took too long.

Perfection is the enemy—good enough is the goal.

That's why I only want you to spend 30 minutes on this, no more. That time-constraint will force you to just get to the point, which is perfect for you.

STEP 1: BRAINSTORM THE CHAPTERS FOR YOUR BOOK (10-MINUTE TIME LIMIT)

The first step in creating your outline is to brainstorm what chapters go in your book.

What's a book chapter? It's essentially a single cohesive idea, fully explored. Depending on how you organize your book, it can be a step in your process, one of several principles, or anything along those lines.

Keep working on your list of chapters—adding, subtracting, moving—until you have the major points you want to explain in the basic order you want to explain them.

Spend no more than 10 minutes on this.

Don't worry too much about the order at this point (it will probably change in the next step). All you want to do here is figure out what you believe your chapters are right now.

Also, don't spend too much time worrying about chapter titles. Just write something down. You can change it later.

While there are numerous ways to brainstorm, there are 2 frameworks that we've found work best:

Framework 1: "Workshop Presentation"

This framework works very well for people used to formally presenting their knowledge. Just imagine that you're giving a speech, presentation, or workshop covering your material.

What would be part 1? What would be part 2? How would you break up the days?

Use the structure of the workshop or presentation as the chapters of your book.

Framework 2: "Teach Your Book to a Client"

For this framework, begin with your ideal reader, the person who would benefit most from your ideas and knowledge. Imagine teaching them everything in your book.

What are the major lessons? What's step 1? Step 2? Write it all down.

If you get stuck in this framework, use your reader as your motivator. Picture your ideal client, friend, or student in your mind: how would you explain your process to them?

What would they get confused about?

What points would they struggle with?

What lessons would you convey to them?

What would they find particularly helpful?

What questions would they ask you?

The beauty of "teaching your book" is that it's an excellent frame for articulating the knowledge you have that you might take for granted.

But before you dive into your brainstorming, here's a quick warning:

I've seen authors begin writing their book in the middle of their brainstorming. They produce pages and pages of content and end up getting frustrated.

Don't go down that rabbit hole. That's why you only get 10 minutes.

Your list of key points and arguments shouldn't run longer than a few pages. If you're writing more than that at this stage, you're going too deep, too soon. Stay at the 30,000-foot level.

Keep your descriptions to short phrases or single sentences so that you're forced to stick to main points. Don't worry about capturing all the details that come to mind. You won't forget what you know. This step is just about clarifying what you know, down to the basics that you want to describe to your reader.

Whichever model you choose, understand that this part of the process can take some time, but don't get too bogged down by it. The point here is to find the major ideas and themes—the chapters. You can always come back and change things later if necessary.

Helpful Note: When you're brainstorming your chapters, have a section of your page called the "parking lot."

Use the parking lot to store all the good ideas you have that don't seem to fit. This will free your mind of any random ideas and keep you focused on the main idea of your book.

While those other ideas might be great, chances are they'll be better suited for future books. Keep them in the parking lot until you need them.

STEP 2: CREATE A TABLE OF CONTENTS (5-MINUTE TIME LIMIT)

Once you've brainstormed your chapters, put them in your Table of Contents, and write the key takeaway for each chapter. This is called a thesis statement.

A thesis statement is a short summation of the main point you want to make in the chapter. *Do not* overwrite these. They should be 1 or 2 sentences each—that's it.

Example Table of Contents

How Many Chapters Should Your Book Have?

Most nonfiction books have between 5 and 20 chapters.

Any less than 5, and your chapters may be running long or may contain too many ideas. More than 20, and you may be including unnecessary content.

There's no "right" answer to this question. But if you do break standard conventions, make sure you're doing it in the best interest of your book and your reader.

STEP 3: PUT IN THE CHAPTER CONTENTS (15-MINUTE TIME LIMIT)

Using the Table of Contents you created, fill in the content for each chapter. You are filling in the main points and stories and examples in your book, and that's it.

Remember: don't write the book in the outline. *The purpose of the outline is to tell you what to write when you sit down to write.*

You should only worry about 2 things:

1. What are the main points you need to make in the chapter?
2. What stories and examples do you want to use?

What Are Main Points?

These are just the main points you want to make in each chapter. You can list these quickly and succinctly, but the outline of the chapter should be laid out fairly well by the time you're done.

It should be ordered in a logical way so that you're building your point or argument like a pyramid. Provide the basic foundational information first, then build up from there.

Don't go too in-depth by writing every detail. If you see you've written paragraphs, you're getting ahead of yourself.

What Are Stories and Examples?

For this section of your outline, list the stories and examples you think you want to share in each chapter.

Effective stories are crucial to the success of a book. They're a great way to make the book and its specific takeaway points more memorable. Many readers forget facts after they read a book, but anecdotes and stories stay with them. They're often more "sticky."

To be clear: this does NOT mean that, in your book, you first write your main points and THEN your stories. Of course, you'll integrate your stories and main points within your chapters.

We recommend separating them in the outline simply because it's not always clear which stories you want to use and where you want to use them. Listing these separately allows you to figure this out as you go.

Chapter Examples

Note: these examples are from different books.

CHAPTER 3: HOW CAN WE IMPROVE PUBLIC HEALTH?

1. CHAPTER THESIS	No other healthcare space can benefit more from the application of anthropology and design thinking than the public health sector.
2. MAIN POINTS	• List the current problems within healthcare • Why design thinking alone is not the solution (every patient requires their own individualized approach) • What does educational assistance look like in public health? • What we can learn from public health experts (What is their process, and what tools do they use?) • How anthropology and design thinking come together to benefit public health
3. STORIES AND EXAMPLES	• Story demonstrating the ramifications of the current problems in healthcare • Example of a time when a patient benefited from an individualized approach

CHAPTER 6: RECRUITERS WILL BE REPLACED BY TECHNOLOGY

1. CHAPTER THESIS

AI will replace millions of jobs, but it will CREATE millions more. Technology will NOT replace recruiters. Rather, it will create more demand for recruiters with the RIGHT SKILLSETS, which is what this chapter is all about.

2. MAIN POINTS

- How to draw the brakes on automating a broken system until the underlying problems are fixed
- What readers need to consider in terms of their process before they go about implementing new technology
- How to develop the kind of skills that technology will never be able to replace

3. STORIES AND EXAMPLES

- Example of a skill that can't be replaced by technology and how it's valuable for recruiters
- Story of how recruiters in a high-profile company have addressed issues in their processes and what positive changes that created

1. CHAPTER THESIS	Once you have a sense of where you are and where you want to go, you have to identify the most important elements for moving a project forward. This chapter helps you prioritize, organize, and create a plan that will get stuff done.
2. MAIN POINTS	• After we know Point A and Point B, we have to figure out how to move us there. • Review all the materials collected. Much of it will come from there. Especially by those doing the work. • Identify priorities based on the most important criteria (What matters most? Speed of implementation? Equity? Effectiveness? Efficiency? Exportability?) • Review leading practices, literature, and talk to those who have done it before. Identify the specific elements of what they did, and determine the extent to which you have implemented them (Harvey balls). • Compare where we are (chapter 1) to leading practices and identify the gaps. • Convene task forces to pull in experts who may be able to intervene in a policy exercise. • Distill all action steps to those that were foundational and required. Those that could wait were scoped into a future phase. • Prioritize. Always prioritize. Credit an order of merit listing. • Interview questions (metrics, tech, success, lessons learned, failures, wish you had known, etc.). • Organize around background, leading practices, implementation roadmap, prioritization, recommendations. • Use the best and the worst and compare. 311 service requests that have a high satisfaction rate compared to those that did not.
3. STORIES AND EXAMPLES	• Flood mitigation task force. After we identified the hotspots and conducted on-the-ground surveys, we then reconvened the task force and brought the team in so we could identify how to leverage City resources to improve the situation. • Operation Enforcement Analytics. After conducting 120 interviews, 20 process flows, ride-alongs, and interviews of the entire process, the needs of the unit were readily apparent.

CHAPTER 5: DOING TOO MUCH

1. CHAPTER THESIS	Stop trying to "multitask" and spread everyone too thin; instead, focus everyone in the company on the "vital few."

2. MAIN POINTS

- What This Means
  - A lot of orgs try to do tons of initiatives in a given year or time frame. This is bad.
  - Reasons why orgs do too much.
    - Changing world/don't want to miss out
    - Need to prove value to someone and more = better
    - Machine gun approach is best
  - Multitasking is bad in personal life. Same in business.
- Common Symptoms for the Diagnosis
  - Duplicate work
  - Departmental conflict
  - No one knows what's the most important thing to prioritize
  - Things get done half-assed and either lobbed over the fence to fail or good ideas stalled and die
  - Wasting time in meetings, getting approvals, or initiatives that start and stop/"hurry up and wait"
  - Stretched resources and missed deadlines
  - Wasted money on things that won't make a big impact
- Treatment
  - Prioritize the vital few at the beginning and at the top (but with input from below), and then stick to your guns and do not change course in spite of temptation
  - Host an executive retreat à la Steve Jobs and Apple. Include details of pre-work from the rest of the org
  - Eliminate siloed goals

3. STORIES AND EXAMPLES

- What This Means
  - Personal story of working in an org that had more than 50 different goals across the company and various siloed functions—just for 1 year!
- Common Symptoms for the Diagnosis
  - Steve Jobs 4 quadrants
- Treatment
  - Slow is smooth; smooth is fast
  - Steve Jobs saying no to 1,000 things
  - My experience—no more than 3-5. Not 10 or more!
  - I've facilitated the Steve Jobs executive retreat and got the best compliment
  - Marcus's story about Apple cutting off projects immediately?

QUESTION: WHY NOT STRUCTURE CHAPTERS LIKE YOU'LL WRITE THEM?

If you have outlining experience, you may notice we don't structure our outline in the traditional way. You might be used to something like this:

1. Major Point 1
   A. Minor Point 1
      I. Story Y
      II. Example Y
   B. Minor Point 2
      I. Story X
      II. Example X
2. Major Point 2
   A. Minor Point 1
      I. Story A
      II. Point B
   B. Minor Point 2
      I. Story A
      II. Point B

There are a few reasons we don't recommend this style of outline:

1. IT DOESN'T WORK WELL.

We've helped thousands of authors position, structure, and write books. By this point, we've tested everything.

We've found that the traditional outline style doesn't work well with most authors. There are several reasons we believe it doesn't work well (the main one is detailed below), but why it doesn't work doesn't matter.

The fact is, it *doesn't* work.

We developed our style of outlining after testing dozens of iterations and discovering what actually produced the best books in the least amount of time.

2. MOST AUTHORS CAN'T GET TO THAT LEVEL OF DETAIL UNTIL THEY START WRITING.

Most authors have trouble understanding precisely how to lay their books out. This is understandable; writing and structuring books is hard and very foreign to people who haven't done it before.

We find that the traditional outline structure gets people lost in the outline. The best way to actually get people writing is to chunk up the chapter into sections. All they need to do is jot down enough so they understand what they're trying to say and what they need to write.

Then they can figure out the details as they write.

3. THIS STYLE KEEPS THE AUTHOR MOVING FORWARD INSTEAD OF GETTING STUCK.

The conventional method of outlining forces authors to get very deep into their knowledge at a stage where some of their ideas may not be worked out yet.

Most people don't do well with a long, detailed outline. They do much better by writing their way to understanding.

This process allows for either approach. You can go into the details if you really want (although I don't recommend it)— or you can just write down the bullet points you need and figure out the rest as you write.

SUMMARY

Outlining a book can be simple for an entrepreneur if you use this fast method that is designed to take no more than 30 minutes.

THE 30-MINUTE BOOK OUTLINE

Step 1: Brainstorm the Chapters for Your Book (10-minute time limit)

The first step in creating your outline is to brainstorm what chapters go in your book. Spend no more than 10 minutes on this.

Step 2: Create a Table of Contents (5-minute time limit)

Once you've brainstormed your chapters, put them in your Table of Contents, and write the key takeaway for each chapter. This is called a thesis statement.

A thesis statement is a short summation of the main point you want to make in the chapter. *Do not* overwrite these. They should be 1 or 2 sentences each—that's it.

Step 3: Put in the Chapter Contents (15-minute time limit)

Using the Table of Contents you created, fill in the content for each chapter. You are filling in the main points and stories and examples in your book, and that's it.

PART 4

WRITE YOUR BOOK (WITHOUT THE PAIN)

There are 4 basic ways to write a book—but for entrepreneurs, there are certain methods that work better than others. Ranked in order from best to worst, these are:

1. Have someone interview you to get your content, but they write it.
2. Write it yourself, with professional guidance.
3. Hire a ghostwriter and have them write it.
4. Write it all by yourself.

I'll go through each one in detail so you can pick the best option for you.

1. GET SOMEONE TO INTERVIEW YOU

This is the best path for most entrepreneurs.

Once you sell yourself on writing a book and do a quick outline to convince yourself that you have a solid book idea in hand, you should use the Who Not How method—and find a Who for your book.

The idea behind this method is very simple: instead of facing a blank page and typing your first draft on your own, you get to turn your ideas into a book by saying them out loud to someone who is interviewing you about them.

The truth is, writing is challenging for most people—and not because they're unintelligent, unskilled, or lazy. It's because writing is a very specialized skill. And writing is completely unrelated to having wisdom, experience, or knowledge to share.

Think about it: how many intelligent and accomplished people do you know who hate writing but have plenty to say?

Quite a few, I'm sure (you might even be one).

Even Julius Caesar, one of the most prolific authors of the Roman Age, used scribes to write nearly all his letters and books. His time was too valuable to be spent mastering the skill of writing. He spent his time thinking and doing things instead.

That's why this method works so well for entrepreneurs; it's easier, faster, and generally makes for better writing.

- Easier: it gets you to a rough draft in about a quarter of the time it would take you to write a first draft.
- Faster: it saves you the time and anxiety of contending with a blank page.
- Makes a better book: it forces you to teach your knowledge in a way that's reader-centric.

You might think I'm biased saying this since I literally started a company that helps people write books with this method.

You'd be right! In fact, that's the reason I started Scribe—it *is* the best method for so many people, *especially* entrepreneurs.

But don't take my word for it. This is what Dan Sullivan says:

> *"Serious entrepreneurs should absolutely hire a great writer to interview them and get their words onto the page.*
>
> *First, it's not your unique ability, so you should find a Who whose unique ability it is, and let them do their job.*
>
> *Second, even if you can write, the best writing actually reads like normal speech. It's direct, personal, and comes across as storytelling. So having your book flow like normal speech will be a major advantage for you, and unless you know how to write that way, it's not easy to do.*
>
> *Third, the recorded interview process is so useful because I've*

noticed that virtually everyone is at their most clear-cut, concise, and articulate when they're answering a question in live conversation. You want to make certain that the questioner really understands and remembers what you are saying. You automatically add the right examples and stories to get your points across. This extra effort to be understood comes across in the writing that results from the conversation."

This is why Dan has been using this process to create books and content for decades—because it works.

Serious and busy entrepreneurs are almost always better off if they can talk about their ideas to a skilled interviewer and writer who can turn those ideas into a book for them.

2. WRITE IT YOURSELF, WITH PROFESSIONAL GUIDANCE

You may not want to be interviewed for various reasons. Writing your book yourself—with the proper guidance—is a valid path. There are many advantages (and disadvantages) to writing it yourself.

Let's start with the advantages. Remember how I said writing is a specialized skill? Well, the only way to get better at it is to practice consistently. There's no better way to do that than by writing a book.

And not only will you develop and hone your writing skills, but you'll also experience a lot of growth—both personally and professionally. That's because writing a book on your own requires enormous self-reflection, and it requires you to learn how to clearly communicate your ideas.

Not to mention, many authors feel an immense sense of ownership once they finish writing their book. That's because you know that *you* were the one who crafted the words. *You* were the one who put in the many hours it took to finish. Writing it on your own, while challenging, is a great source of pride and confidence.

But despite the many advantages of writing a book yourself, there are also clear disadvantages to consider.

The most obvious is time.

Writing a book is a very time-consuming endeavor. There's simply no way around it—you have to put in the work. At best, writing your first draft will take several months. At worst, it will take several years.

You need to ask yourself how much your time is worth to you. Is it best spent writing out your book on your own? Or are there more efficient ways to use that time?

This leads to the mental obstacles you'll likely have to overcome when writing your book. If it takes longer than you anticipated or is harder than you expected, you're likely going to get frustrated. Or worse, you'll lose confidence in your ability and stall out.

That's why, if you decide you want to write the book yourself, I highly recommend you do so with professional guidance. Having an experienced book coach to turn to during the writing process will help you navigate and overcome those obstacles.

They can provide the guidance, accountability, and help that will allow you to finish your book in a timely manner (with your confidence intact).

So how exactly *do* you write your book?

First, you make a plan.

CREATE A WRITING PLAN

It took me 3 years as a professional writer before I understood that I needed a writing plan for every book I wrote. Writing without a plan is like driving across the country without a map. Sure, you might get there, but it'll take you at least twice as long.

A writing plan is crucial—I can't emphasize that enough.

It defines exactly what you'll do to finish your book. It lays out when and where you're going to write each day, how much you'll write, when everything is due, and how you'll keep yourself accountable. And all it takes is 5 simple steps:

1. Schedule a time and place to write each day.

Be as specific as possible, but don't overthink it. Write wherever and whenever you work best. I recommend setting aside at least 1 hour per day, but if you can only write 6 days a week or 30 minutes per day, that's fine. The key here is to establish consistency that translates into momentum.

2. Set specific writing goals.

I recommend a goal of 250 words per hour of writing. It may seem like a low bar, but that's the point. Reaching that goal every day will motivate you to continue. Plus, it adds up quickly. By writing just 250 words a day, you can get a 120-page (30,000-word) first draft done in about 4 months.

3. Build deadlines.

Deadlines force action and demand accountability. Depending on how fast you want to go and how busy you are, you can set a deadline to finish 1 chapter every 1–3 weeks.

4. Announce the book.

Announcing that you're writing a book is the best way to hold yourself accountable. Plus, you'll get a lot of positive feedback, which will motivate you to start. Choose whichever platform has the most people on it that you care about, and announce it there.

5. Keep yourself accountable.

Post daily updates of your writing progress online or share it with a select group of people in a private group. It doesn't matter where you post updates, as long as you're sharing them with others. Doing this will compel you to meet your daily writing goal, and the encouragement you'll receive will keep you going.

This is the framework my company has used with thousands of authors, and it works extremely well. I don't know of any other method that provides better results. That said, the important thing here is to do what works best for you. If something in this plan doesn't work well for you, adjust it as needed.

Once you've finalized your plan, it's time to sit down and write.

HOW TO WRITE THE FIRST DRAFT OF YOUR BOOK

After working with thousands of authors, I've found that the majority know how to write out their ideas. What they need most is to identify their audience and establish a clear writing plan. Once they do that, the writing itself is relatively simple.

Where problems arise is in the mindset around writing. That's when authors get stuck. There's a very simple way to avoid this:

Give yourself permission to write a mediocre first draft.

Most first-time authors have this notion that professional writers put out amazing first drafts; they believe that their first draft has to be exceptional. That's absurd.

I can tell you, as a professional writer who has written 4 *New York Times* bestsellers and someone who has seen early drafts of many massive bestsellers, that everyone's first drafts are utter garbage.

Mine especially. Worse than mediocre. They're terrible. But that doesn't bother me because I know I can edit them until they're not terrible. Barbara Kingsolver put it best:

"1. To begin, give yourself permission to write a bad book.

2. Revise until it's not a bad book."

Many people struggle with giving themselves permission to write a mediocre first draft. That's why we developed a concept called the "vomit draft."

Yes, we literally call the first draft the "vomit draft."

When you're vomiting, you don't care about looking good; you just want to get it all out because that's the only way to get it over with. Same thing with a vomit draft—just get it out and get it over with.

What's great about the vomit draft is, unlike vomiting in front of people, your vomit draft is ONLY for you. You're the only person who will ever see it, and you'll edit it before even your editor sees it.

If you only focus on getting the words out, you won't read and edit as you go (which would inevitably slow you down). When you write something you think is garbage, just say, "That's a problem for future me!" and keep moving.

This is important:

Write your vomit draft as quickly as possible. Don't stop. Don't edit. Move forward without looking back until your vomit draft is done.

Let me repeat that: Write your vomit draft as quickly as possible.

DO NOT STOP TO READ IT.

DO NOT EDIT.

KEEP WRITING UNTIL YOUR VOMIT DRAFT IS DONE.

I cannot be more serious or literal about this. The quickest way to derail a vomit draft is to start editing before you finish. I don't care who you are—if you start editing your vomit draft, you *will* get stuck.

Plus, if you edit during the vomit draft stage, you'll double the amount of time it takes to write the book—and that's the best-case scenario.

Using the Vomit Draft Method does 2 things:

1. It suspends your self-judgment.
2. It creates momentum through daily victories (even writing just 250 words per day is cause for celebration, and it reframes how you see yourself).

If you edit as you write, you'll derail your book. The bully in your brain, the part of you that's ridiculously hard on yourself, will start to second-guess you. It will shame you and will, at best, slow you down—if not kill your motivation altogether.

USE GOOD WRITING PRINCIPLES

Remember writing essays in school with a minimum word count?

If you were like me, you were guilty of turning "they said" into "they then proceeded to vocally exclaim..."

I can't think of a worse way to learn to write.

I didn't have 5 pages of thoughts about Paul Revere's ride, but being forced to write that much forced me to write convoluted sentences packed with unnecessary words in order to pad my essay and hit the space requirement.

What I didn't learn in school is how to write something people want to read. That's the key to nonfiction, and it's never covered in school.

Great nonfiction is short, simple, direct, and about the reader. Follow these principles, and your writing will improve exponentially.

1. Make it short.

This is the most important principle. If you get this one right, the rest (usually) take care of themselves.

Keep your writing short on all levels. Short chapters (usually no more than 4K words). Short paragraphs (2–3 sentences). Short sentences (5–20 words). Even shorter words (less than 12 characters).

Brevity forces economy and effectiveness. When you put a space constraint on your writing, it compels you to focus on the essentials and cut the rest.

Still, many authors struggle with the idea of having a "little" book. But let me be the first to assure you, having a short book is *great*.

I'll tell you why:

A "little" book is much more persuasive in the 21st century than a big book.

Nobody has the attention span to figure out what you're trying to tell them anymore. With the proliferation of TV and the internet, the world's tolerance for lengthy communications has dropped off a cliff. If you can't grab their attention in the first few minutes, you've lost them.

I'm no exception. If I'm not interested in the first minute, I'll probably change the channel or click on another site.

The truth is that nobody cares about you or what you're trying to sell. The only thing your readers are thinking about is how they can make their personal future bigger, better, more exciting, and more meaningful.

They want new ideas, new strategies, and new methods that are better than anything they're currently using. That's the only thing they'll be interested in when they pick up your book.

You don't need a 200-page book to give that to them.

So don't waste their time, attention, interest, and goodwill by writing about anything except them and their transformed future.

That said, make it as short as possible without leaving anything out. Short does not mean missing essential content.

2. Make it simple.

Simple is very similar to short, but *not* the same thing. You can write something that's short but complex—but that doesn't work well.

Of course, it's okay if your ideas are complex. But even

complex ideas can be broken down into small words and short sentences. Doing this forces you to write in plain English, which makes it easier for your readers to understand you.

As Richard Feynman said, if you cannot explain your idea simply, it probably means you don't fully understand it (which is bad if you're writing a book).

3. Make it direct.

Most nonfiction writing is indirect in some way—passive voice, jargon, multiple clauses, heavy use of adjectives and adverbs, etc.

Don't do these things. If you're doing them, stop.

If you aren't sure what they are, then do this:

Make each sentence a single, clear statement. Connect it to the sentence before and the sentence after. Do not put multiple thoughts in 1 sentence.

Essentially, make your writing as direct as possible.

Also, pay attention to passive and active voice. Most people don't know the difference between them, but understanding it can have a big impact on your writing.

Active voice means the subject of the sentence is performing the action. Passive voice means the subject of the sentence receives the action. Even though they mean the same thing, the effect is very different. For example:

Active: Tucker *wrote* the book.

Passive: The book *was written by* Tucker.

Active voice is much easier for people to read because they can visualize the sentence. You can see Tucker writing a book.

But with passive voice, there's another cognitive step involved. You have to first imagine a book, *then* think about Tucker writing that book.

This small cognitive step makes a huge difference in how people respond to your writing.

4. Make it about the reader.

Ask yourself this question about everything you write:

Why does the reader care?

This is the hardest principle to apply because when you do this, you realize that most of your writing is for yourself—

not the reader. You see your writing for what it probably is: selfish, indulgent, and grandiose.

If that happens, don't get down on yourself. It's very common. Nearly every author in the world has had that problem. All you have to do is stop writing about things the reader doesn't care about and focus on what they do.

HOW TO EDIT THE FIRST DRAFT OF YOUR BOOK

Once your vomit draft is complete, you can move on to the self-editing process. But before you do that, take some time to rest and relax.

I'm serious.

Set the entire draft aside for at least a week, ideally 2. This will give you a valuable, fresh perspective when you come back and begin editing.

Once you're rested and are ready to start editing, keep this idea in mind as you comb through your draft:

The book isn't for you—it's for your reader.

Let me explain.

Of course the book is yours, and it has your ideas—no one

will dispute that. But if you want the book to help you, then it must provide value to the reader. In essence, to get what you want, you must give them what they want.

With this in mind, you're ready to start self-editing. There are 2 steps I recommend:

1. **The "Line-by-Line" Edit:** Go deep into the chapters, paragraphs, and sentences to make sure it says exactly what you want.
2. **The "Read-Aloud" Edit:** Read the manuscript out loud—preferably to a person—and make sure it sounds right to the ear.

DO THE "LINE-BY-LINE" EDIT

This is the framework we use at Scribe for our line-by-line editing. It's simple to understand, but powerful if you do it right. It gives you the exact questions to ask yourself at each level of editing.

As you read every chapter, ask yourself these 5 questions:

1. What point am I making?
2. Is it necessary?
3. Is it as short as possible?
4. Is it as simple as possible?
5. Is it as direct as possible?

I mean this literally—ask yourself these questions each time.

Yes, this is tedious. But if you do this exercise consistently, it becomes second nature. Once that happens, you'll find that you not only can cut the fluff out of your book, but you can also make your book sharper and more refined. You'll be able to hone in on what you're trying to say and nail it.

Do it for each paragraph, then do it for each sentence. If you do this, you'll have an excellent book.

And don't be afraid to cut as much as possible. As Stephen King says,

> "When your story is ready for rewrite, cut it to the bone. Get rid of every ounce of excess fat. This is going to hurt; revising a story down to the bare essentials is always a little like murdering children, but it must be done."

DO THE "READ-ALOUD" EDIT

This is an editing process that's not commonly taught, but it's a secret trick of numerous bestselling authors. Brené Brown, Neil Strauss, myself—we all do this.

When I wrote my first book, I had teams of proofreaders working on it. I didn't think a single mistake would sneak by, and I happily locked in the manuscript.

A few months later, I recorded my audiobook, and as I read through the manuscript out loud, I was *horrified.*

There were hundreds of tiny little mistakes that I only noticed after saying them out loud. Not just spelling errors—there were very few of those. These were mostly word choice or phrasing mistakes.

It drove me NUTS.

Don't make the mistake I made. Read your manuscript out loud and mark changes as you go.

If the words roll off your tongue, they'll also flow smoothly in readers' heads. Because I waited until so late in the process to read it out loud, it was too late to make edits to the book.

Learn from my mistake. Read your manuscript out loud, and make your changes before you start the publishing process.

If you find it difficult to take the time to read out loud (and a lot of authors do), I recommend having a friend help you out. If someone is sitting in the room with you, listening as you read through the manuscript, it'll create the social pressure you need to actually do it.

If it's something you would say out loud, then it will read

clearly on the page. If it's something you would never say to another person, it won't read as clearly.

The reason reading your manuscript out loud works so well is because you'll catch dozens of things you would have otherwise missed. Hearing yourself speak forces you to notice bad or strange phrasings—even if you don't know *why* it's off, you know it's off.

If possible, read each chapter to a person. I know, it sounds awful and tedious, but reading to actual people forces you to really hear what is and isn't working. It's an incredible forcing function.

If you can't do that, then set up a microphone and record yourself as you read aloud. You can delete the recording afterward. All that matters is that you're reading it *out loud*.

This is key to making this process work.

When you listen to what your words are saying—you'll hear the errors.

3. HIRE A GHOSTWRITER AND HAVE THEM DO EVERYTHING

Hiring a ghostwriter can work as well, but it has major drawbacks. Before you consider this option, be aware of the following:

1. HIRING A GHOSTWRITER IS EXPENSIVE.

A ghostwriter is a major investment. It will cost you anywhere from $25,000 to $250,000+. Any ghostwriter who charges under $25,000 is bottom of the barrel. At best, they're just bad writers. At worst, they're flat-out plagiarizing other people's work.

If you can't afford more than $25,000 for a ghostwriter, you shouldn't hire one. Professional ghostwriters with credits and reputation will usually charge between $25,000 and $75,000. This varies depending on their level of expertise, the amount of work required for the project, and how much work they're currently juggling.

Generally speaking, a proven and reliable ghostwriter with many good references will charge at least $40K for a book (and usually more).

Once you get into the 6-figure realm, you're talking about a very small number of well-established authors with extensive experience ghostwriting bestsellers (they often have books out under their own names that are well-respected).

2. BUSINESS GHOSTWRITERS ARE HARD TO FIND AND HIRE.

If you want to buy a book, you can go to Amazon and find it for the best price. It's a transparent, reliable marketplace for books.

There's no equivalent transparent, reliable marketplace for ghostwriters.

In order to find a ghostwriter, you'll have to look in many different places, and each one will have different people listed at different prices. And unless you're skilled at hiring and testing writers, you'll have trouble evaluating them.

Even if you find one you want, you then have to negotiate a deal and set all the proper expectations. If you don't know how to do that, it's going to be a very difficult process.

3. BUSINESS GHOSTWRITERS CAN BE DIFFICULT TO MANAGE.

Finding and hiring a ghostwriter is just the first step. Are you a good manager? Especially of someone you don't know, working in a field you don't know well? Because that's going to be necessary if you hire a ghostwriter.

After you hire them, the relationship changes. Their selfish goal is to get the work done as fast as possible and get you out the door, so they can sign their next client.

Remember, they're a freelancer. The only way they make money is by signing authors to contracts.

If you pick a good ghostwriter, this won't be much of an issue—they'll do a good job, even if they do it quickly.

But if you don't, you'll have to worry about missed deadlines, payment issues, conflicts, poor work product, and any number of other issues that come from managing a freelance contractor who's looking for their next project.

4. THERE ARE NO GUARANTEES IN GHOSTWRITING.

The only thing you can be sure of with ghostwriting is that it's expensive. You can't get guarantees of quality or reliability—or get your money back.

Even if you spend a lot of money, you're doing it in the hope that it'll work, not on a guarantee that it'll work. You can't get a guarantee because you're not paying for a manuscript— you're paying for the ghostwriter's time.

If the ghostwriters allowed for "money-back guarantee" or "quality guarantee" clauses, they'd be setting themselves up for endless revisions with authors. It could mean thousands of hours of work. Since these writers literally make their money by selling their time, they can't do that.

I don't want to make it sound like they're out to cheat you. That's not true. In fact, most of them are good people who like working on books, and they want to do a good job.

The problem is that some authors are totally unreasonable. As a result, ghostwriters have to structure their deals this way to protect themselves from the few really bad clients out there.

5. THERE'S NO PROCESS WITH GHOSTWRITING.

This is the heart of the issue: ghostwriting has no defined process. Each ghostwriter has their own personal system, so you can't know at any given stage what's going on, how well it's going, etc. You're completely in the hands of the ghostwriter you're working with.

These are all the ways ghostwriting can go wrong that can't really be guaranteed against:

- You're a bad match with your writer.
- Your writer delivers a bad manuscript.
- There's no defined process to rely on, so you can't check the work of the ghostwriter ahead of time; you have to hope they can get it done right.
- There's no centralized authority to appeal to.

This is a *lot* of risk.

That's why the best ghostwriters are so expensive—the more money you spend, and the more experience and reputation the ghostwriter has, the lower the risk.

6. YOU'RE NOT THE (TRUE) AUTHOR OF YOUR OWN BOOK.

This is possibly the biggest negative, at least for most people.

It might seem shocking to an honest person, but many authors who use ghostwriters don't actually know much about the subject of their book. They have some ideas and some things they know, but they hired the ghostwriter so they don't have to do the hard work of coming up with the ideas or expressing those ideas.

That's why many people have a low opinion of ghostwriting.

This is especially important to note for business books. Part of the reason you're writing the book is because you're saying that the book contains your unique knowledge. If it doesn't in fact contain that, then there's a major trust issue.

Ultimately, the decision to hire a ghostwriter is up to your discretion. While it can save you time and ensure that your book is completed, it's also a costly method that has no guarantees.

Only hire a ghostwriter if you know the risks involved and can make the investment necessary for an experienced professional.

Note: I am differentiating between hiring a writer to interview you and hiring a ghostwriter. This is because I see them as very different. Some people may not, but in my experience, hiring a writer/company who knows how to interview you and write a book of those interviews—that you then edit—is very different than hiring a pure ghostwriter.

4. WRITE IT ALL ALONE

This is the worst thing you can do, and for most people, it guarantees failure.

Writing a book is hard enough *with* guidance, accountability, and help.

To do it without these things is not just difficult—it's beyond the desire or capability of most people.

It also doesn't make sense if you're an entrepreneur. Why would you spend time learning this yourself when you can make it much easier?

SUMMARY

There are 4 ways to write your book:

1. HAVE SOMEONE INTERVIEW YOU TO GET YOUR CONTENT, BUT THEY WRITE IT.

Most entrepreneurs should do this. It's the quickest, best

way to ensure that your book is good and that it gets done with the least amount of effort from you.

2. WRITE IT YOURSELF, WITH PROFESSIONAL GUIDANCE.

This works as well; it just takes more time and effort, but can be worth the cost to some entrepreneurs.

3. HIRE A GHOSTWRITER AND HAVE THEM WRITE IT.

This can work but can be a bit sketchy, because of specific problems with ghostwriters.

4. WRITE IT ALL BY YOURSELF.

This is the worst choice by far.

PART 5

THE ENTREPRENEUR'S TRICK TO QUICKLY AND EASILY PUBLISHING A BOOK

Let me be very clear and up front about this:

You should not self-publish; you need to use a professional to publish your book for you.

This is regardless of how you wrote it, and it is especially true for entrepreneurs.

Why?

Because it isn't your unique ability. Thus, spending your effort on it will be a huge waste of your time.

But—and this is very important—don't pay just anyone. That's why I said "professional."

Publishing professionals are experts for a reason. You can count on them to make you and your book look as good as possible.

1. WHY ENTREPRENEURS SHOULD PROFESSIONALLY PUBLISH

There's more to publishing than simply binding your pages together and making them available for purchase.

Professional publishing is a multifaceted, intricate process. It requires you to take your manuscript through dozens of steps and checkpoints before it gets anywhere close to a final, published product.

But let me be clear: when I say professional publishing, I'm *not* referring to traditional publishing houses. It's no longer necessary to work with traditional publishers, and in fact, I don't recommend it for most entrepreneurs (I explain why below).

And, as I mentioned, I also don't recommend attempting it all on your own (what most people call self-publishing). Navigating each stage of the self-publishing process solo would require all of your time and attention—and you *still* wouldn't have a high-quality end product.

Instead, the best option for entrepreneurs is to hire a professional publishing firm.

In order to position your book as well as possible (and ensure that it's successful), you'll need professionals to guide you through the process *and* make sure your book looks good when it's done.

At a minimum, a high-quality professional publishing firm can help you with the following:

MANUSCRIPT EVALUATION AND QUALITY ASSURANCE

Professional publishing firms will tell you exactly what steps are needed to make your manuscript ready for publication.

For example, at Scribe, we have editors who provide our authors with an overview of their manuscripts' strengths and areas of concern. They also execute a full copyedit and proofread, so authors can be sure that their book will positively reflect on them.

BOOK COVER DESIGN

Designing the book cover is a crucial part of the publication process. You want to make sure that it accurately reflects the content of your book—*and* that it will engage potential readers.

Anyone who's ever held a book in their hands understands how important the cover is. As much as we don't want to admit it, everyone judges a book by its cover. So unless you're a graphic designer, book covers are best left to the professionals.

Most professional publishing firms have in-house or freelance designers who work specifically on covers. At Scribe, we've hired designers who are quite literally some of the best in the world—because we know how important it is.

INTERIOR LAYOUT

Have you ever started to read a book, and on the first page—before engaging with the actual content—you immediately get a bad feeling and can't take the book seriously? *And you can't even explain why?*

That's the impact of the book's layout. Despite how simple it seems (or perhaps because of it), book layout is one of the major factors that separates amateurish books from professional ones.

It's not easy to format the interior layout of a book. In fact, working with type is considered the most difficult thing to do in design. But if you want to create a cohesive visual experience for your reader from the cover to the final page, you'll need to get it right.

Professional publishing firms can make sure you don't fall victim to a bad layout.

PRINTING AND DISTRIBUTION

A professional publishing firm can help print and distribute your book to all major platforms, such as Amazon and Barnes & Noble. This includes paperback, hardcover, *and* eBook versions.

While it's technically possible to do this on your own, distribution and printing can be very complicated and tedious processes. And as is the case with every other part of your book, you want to get it right.

But you don't need to spend an unnecessary amount of time trying to figure it out on your own. Professional firms can take care of those details for you so that you can focus on matters that are more important to you and your business.

THE BOTTOM LINE

There are many other minute steps in the professional publishing process that lead up to printing and distribution. These are just a few of the main essentials. But even this high-level overview should prove to you what I've already stated:

Hiring professionals is necessary if you want to publish a successful book.

2. WHY ENTREPRENEURS SHOULD AVOID TRADITIONAL PUBLISHING

When most people think of the publishing industry, they typically think of the traditional publishing model.

In traditional publishing, an author must find a book agent to represent them to publishing companies. Then, along with the agent, they have to pitch a book publishing company with their book idea.

If the pitch is successful, and the publishing company offers the author a publishing deal, the publishing company purchases the ownership of the print license from the author in return for an advance on royalties (that the author doesn't have to pay back). The author is on their own to write the book, sometimes with editorial help from the publisher, sometimes not.

The publisher then manages and controls the whole publishing and distribution process.

While this model works well for a select group of people (celebs and professional writers), it's *not* a good option for most entrepreneurs.

Let me break it down for you.

IT'S EXTREMELY DIFFICULT TO GET A TRADITIONAL PUBLISHING DEAL

First, it's very difficult to get a traditional publishing deal. There's almost no reason for an entrepreneur to waste their valuable time trying to do it.

To get a publishing deal from a traditional publisher, you must go through these steps:

1. Find a book agent willing to represent you and your book idea to a publisher (this is very hard; most agents get hundreds of inbound requests a week).
2. Write a book proposal (this is such a big task, authors often pay freelance writers $10K–15K or more to do this for them).
3. Shop the book proposal around to publishers (through the agent).
4. Have the publisher actually make you an offer.

Getting the deal is the hardest part of a very hard process. The book publisher's decision typically hinges on one simple fact:

Do you have an existing audience that's waiting to buy a lot of copies of your book?

The reason for this is that traditional publishers are terrible at selling and marketing books. They now rely almost exclusively on authors to do this for them.

If you have an audience, they want to give you a deal because then they know they can make money off of you.

If you don't have a built-in audience—people who follow you and are used to buying things from you already and want your book—then you have almost no shot at getting a deal.

YOU'LL HAVE NO OWNERSHIP OF RIGHTS AND PROFITS

A traditional publishing company always owns the print license (which includes digital), while the author always owns the copyright. All other rights (movie, excerpt, etc.) are negotiable.

This means the publishing company has final say over all aspects of your book.

Not only are you selling the upside profits of your book to the publisher—you're selling them control of your intellectual property.

In fact, publishing companies usually have the absolute right to change your content and writing as they wish. This is part of what they're buying with their money.

Once they own the book, they *only* care about selling copies. You can no longer do anything with that book that doesn't involve paying *them* for copies of it, because that's how publishing companies make money.

YOU LOSE CREATIVE AND CONTENT CONTROL

Make no mistake about this: once you take a deal from a publisher, they own the book and all the content in it, so they get to decide everything that goes into the book. They get final say over the words, the book cover, the author bio—*everything*.

I can tell you from my experience that, as a group, publishers tend to make terrible aesthetic decisions. There are many reasons for this, but the biggest is what I call "adverse selection."

Though some people who work in publishing are deeply skilled and thoughtful editors whose work makes books much better, those people are rare. They tend to only work with the biggest authors.

Many of the people working at publishing companies are doing so because they weren't good enough to make a living as a writer.

I don't say that as a put-down. I say it simply so you understand that someone who didn't make good-enough decisions about their own writing is now in a position to hold final decision-making power over your book.

YOU LOSE MARKETING CONTROL (AND GET NO SUPPORT)

Most publishers do (basically) no marketing.

I can't emphasize this enough—publishers expect YOU to do all the work of selling the book for THEM.

They don't have a plan to sell 25K copies of your book. That's *your* job.

That might be okay for a novelist with a big existing audience, but as an entrepreneur, you want your book to promote you or your business. Working with a traditional publisher greatly restricts your options to do that.

For example, if you want to position yourself as an expert in your field, what happens if they don't think your book topic appeals to enough people?

Traditional publishers don't care about your business. They only care about selling copies of books. Thus, they'll make you go broader with your topic, which means the book won't be as appealing to the specific audience you're trying to reach.

Even worse, because traditional publishers only make money by selling copies of the book, you can't give away copies for free. You can't even give away the PDF for free. And you certainly can't use your content in other places as a lead generator for your company.

They're going to force you to put all your promotion efforts on selling copies, which doesn't always help you reach as many people as possible.

Also, they give you zero price control, so your ability to make marketing deals with any number of people is gone. This type of flexibility is critically important for many aspects of marketing, but they won't do it.

IT'S A HUGE TIME INVESTMENT

Even if you get a traditional book deal, it's a huge amount of effort to put it all together. You have to find an agent to represent you to a traditional publisher, you have to do a book proposal that will appeal to a publisher, and then you have to shop the book deal.

From start to finish, it usually takes 24 months to publish your book—often 36. That's 2 to 3 *years*, which is an incredibly long time in the modern media world, especially for a nonfiction author.

THE BOTTOM LINE

When it comes down to it, traditional publishing provides very little benefit to most entrepreneurs. And unless you're a professional writer, celebrity, politician, or someone with a substantially large audience, chances are you won't get a deal anyway.

Traditional publishing is essentially just a status game. It doesn't get most entrepreneurs much of anything beyond significance.

You're much better off working with a professional publishing firm. Not only will it save you vast amounts of time, but it will allow you to own your intellectual property and use your book as a lead generator for your business (among many other things).

If you decide later that you want to try the traditional route, you can always go back to it.

But take it from me—traditional publishing is better left alone (again, for most entrepreneurs).

3. WHAT MAKES A BOOK PROFESSIONALLY PUBLISHED?

You don't need to be an expert to tell whether a book has been professionally published. You just need to ask yourself one simple question:

When you're holding the book, does it look, read, and feel like any of the great books you've read?

If the answer is yes, chances are it's the work of a professional. It's that simple.

But while it's easy to say that, it's very hard to do.

That's why, when most people say negative things about self-publishing, they're talking about books that look low-quality.

And they're right. Books that look bad don't sell.

Let me lay it out for you in the starkest terms possible:

Almost every potential reader will decide whether or not to buy your book, and what they think of the book, before they've read a single word inside the book.

After a ton of empirical research and decades of experience in the book business, we've developed a clear picture of what happens in readers' minds when judging a book.

But even though we have a good map of how people decide to buy a book (which I'll outline in a moment), you must understand a key insight: *this process is almost never conscious.*

These buying decisions are a series of instantaneous and mostly subconscious judgments. They're made in less than 60 seconds, and they're made together, each influencing the other.

The reader often doesn't know (or believe) they're evaluating the book this way—but they are. These judgments are real and substantive; in most cases, they're the main evaluation and purchase triggers.

That's why professional guidance is crucial when publishing your book. Any professional worth their salt knows how to position your book according to these buying decisions.

A potential reader will consider these pieces of information about your book, (usually) in this order:

1. The title
2. The recommending source
3. The cover
4. The book description
5. The blurbs (aka endorsements)
6. The customer reviews

7. The author bio and picture (depending on where the picture is placed)
8. The length of the book
9. The price (though this can come sooner)
10. The book text itself (the "Look Inside" function online)

TITLE

Most people believe the cover is the first thing readers judge. But that's only true if they're browsing a physical bookstore, which is rarely the case anymore. Most books are now discovered either through word of mouth or online.

In both cases, what's the first piece of information they receive?

The title.

From the title alone, people instantaneously assess whether the book seems relevant and interesting. That's why I recommend you spend a lot of time ensuring that you get the title right.

Let me be clear: A good title *won't* make your book do well, but a bad title will almost certainly *prevent* it from doing so. Many potential readers stop considering a book after only hearing a bad title and nothing else.

RECOMMENDING SOURCE

If Marc Andreessen or Bill Gates recommend a book, thousands of people will rush out to buy it. But if a random person on Twitter with no followers recommends it, no one will rush out to buy it.

This is because the *credibility of the source* is a hugely important piece of the recommendation puzzle. In most cases, people will transfer the credibility of the recommender onto the book.

It's all about *who* is doing the recommending. This applies to friends as well. If you have a friend who's rich, successful, and intelligent, you're far more likely to listen to their book recommendation than the recommendation of a friend who's unemployed and living with his parents.

What's great about this is that if the credibility of the referrer is great enough, almost any title will work, and you don't have to worry about the rest of this list. But that's rarely the case.

BOOK COVER

If the reader is still interested after hearing the title and taking the referring source into account, they'll go to Amazon (or in rare instances, a bookstore) and look at the book.

Once they see the cover, they'll further judge whether the book is interesting and relevant (remember: *people only care about what a book will do for them*).

The most important thing at this point is to not repel the reader. Most people are looking for reasons NOT to buy the book. Don't give them any.

BOOK DESCRIPTION

If the cover hasn't repelled the reader, they'll look at the book description on the Amazon page (or on the back of the book, if they're in a bookstore).

A good book description will give the reader a strong sense of what the book is about. It should make it interesting, but not give everything away.

BLURBS

If the reader is still interested, they'll look at the endorsements (sometimes for a physical book, they'll do this prior to reading the book description).

Note that most readers look more closely at *who* the blurbs are from rather than what they say. They assume that the blurbs will be positive, so they want to see the social status of the blurber and whether it's someone they know and respect.

While blurbs are nice to have, they're not a requirement for a successful book. Just be aware that readers will subconsciously (or consciously) judge your book based on who the blurbs come from.

READER REVIEWS

If the reader is on Amazon (or any other online bookseller), it's guaranteed that they'll look at the customer reviews.

Usually, they'll note the number of total reviews first—as a gauge of popularity—and then look at the average rating. They may then browse the content of the reviews.

If they do check the content of the reviews, they typically read (or more likely scan) 1 or 2 of them. And if they're like most people, they skip the positive reviews and read a negative review before going back to a positive one (if they even do that).

AUTHOR BIO AND PHOTO

Occasionally readers will look at the author's bio and photo. This is usually in situations where they haven't quite made up their mind, and they want more information before deciding to buy the book.

Looking at the author page helps them understand the credibility and relative status of the author.

There are certain cases where this is one of the first things the reader looks at (usually when they've never heard of the author). It depends largely on the reader and their preferences.

But by this point, the vast majority of people have made their decision. And like I pointed out earlier, this is before they've interacted with *anything* inside the book.

They have yet to read one single page, and they've already decided whether or not to buy the book.

LENGTH

This is one of those things that appears to be generational or divided by socioeconomic status.

Some people, generally voracious readers, never think to check the length of a book, whereas others always check. It depends largely on the person. However, most people don't want to commit to 300+ pages.

There's not much you can do here—your book is the length it is—but our data has shown that nonfiction books between 100 and 200 pages sell the best (and are read the most).

PRICE

Some people look at the price when deciding to buy a book.

Book pricing can be both very simple and incredibly complex; it all depends on how deep into the details you dive.

In my experience, readers are far more price-conscious for eBooks than they are for physical books. This is because of value perception. Most people perceive physical books as higher-value items than eBooks.

At the same time, pricing a book too low can hurt your credibility with your readers.

Generally speaking, I recommend keeping your goals for your book in mind when you set your price. Remember, selling copies isn't the only measure of your book's success.

THE BOOK TEXT AND INTERIOR LAYOUT

There are some people who use the "Look Inside" function on Amazon. They want to check out the first few pages and engage with the content of the book itself. If they're in a bookstore, they flip the book open and read a bit. They might even do more research to find articles online about the book.

These are the high-information buyers, but they're a distinct minority. Fewer than 10% of your buyers will do what everyone says they want to do: judge a book by the content inside and not the cover.

4. WHAT DOES IT COST TO PROFESSIONALLY PUBLISH?

If you're like many of the authors I've worked with, you're probably concerned about how cheaply you can publish.

There's nothing wrong with wanting to save money, but you need to remember: your book will be used as a credential to increase your authority, raise your visibility, and expand your career.

Thus, *you simply cannot afford to publish your book cheaply.*

If you do, it will make you and your business look bad. Saving money is great, but never at the expense of putting out a poor product with your name on it.

If this is a concern, there are 2 questions you must answer before you can determine how much it costs to publish a book:

1. What is the value of your time?
2. How professional do you want the book to be?

THE VALUE OF YOUR TIME

Time is an incredibly important factor for any entrepreneur. Your time is extremely valuable, and you need to consider the opportunity costs associated with it.

Opportunity cost is a simple business concept. It means that in addition to the direct cost of an action, there's also a cost in terms of lost opportunity. You must factor in both when calculating the total cost.

Let's stick with book publishing as an example.

If you have a retail job that pays $10 an hour, then the opportunity cost of your time is $10 per hour. But if you have a career that pays you $250,000 a year, you make $125 an hour (given a normal 40-hour workweek). So the opportunity cost of your time would be $125 per hour.

This difference fundamentally changes the calculation for the true cost of publishing a book.

For the sake of example, let's say you have 2 options for publishing your book:

1. You can do everything related to publishing your book on your own (over the course of 100 hours of work), OR
2. You can pay someone else to do it for $10,000 (and spend no time working on it)

For the person making $10 an hour, the choice is clear: 100 hours of work is worth $1,000 to them, which is much cheaper than paying $10,000 to someone else. Therefore, they should do it themselves.

For the person making $250,000 a year ($125/hr), it doesn't make sense to do it on their own. For them, 100 hours of work is worth $12,500. They'll actually *save* $2,500 by hiring someone at $10,000, not to mention that they will make the book MUCH better than if they do it themselves.

Opportunity cost can be tricky to calculate if you're looking to be precise, but it's fairly simple to ballpark. The point is not to have exact numbers, but to understand the value of your time.

As a general rule, you should spend your time where you create the most value for yourself, and for most entrepreneurs, that is NOT working on the publishing aspects of your book.

THE QUALITY: PEOPLE JUDGE YOU BASED ON YOUR BOOK

Most informational pieces about the costs of publishing give you the cheapest methods. That's not a plausible path for entrepreneurs. If you have a professional reputation to uphold, using cheap services to publish your book will actually hurt you.

The fact is, readers will judge your book. And not just the book—they will judge you as a person based on the quality of your book. This is one of those unpleasant but true facts of life. We all say, "You shouldn't judge a book by its cover," but we all do. The more you accept this fact and adapt to it, the better your book—and thus your career—will be.

When evaluating cost, the metric a professional should be using is *quality*. How you can get high quality at a low cost, NOT how you can get the lowest cost possible.

Before you start to panic about price, let me preface it by saying it's not necessary to pay for the best available services at every point in the publishing process. Sometimes acceptable is good enough. The key is knowing where and when to save money and where to spend it. That way, you can make sure you get the highest leverage for your money.

To help you understand this, I'll go through each publishing stage and explain the price ranges for each quality tier: Low Quality, Acceptable, High Quality, and Best Possible.

A WORD ON WRITING COST

This isn't technically part of the publishing process, but it's something you'll need to consider. Writing is one of those areas that can range anywhere from $0 (not counting opportunity cost, of course) to well into 6 figures.

The question you need to ask yourself is whether you want help, and if so, what kind of help you want.

As I mentioned earlier, there are 4 options to consider when writing your book:

1. Have someone interview you to get all the content, but have them write it.
2. Write it yourself, with professional guidance.
3. Hire a ghostwriter and have them do everything.
4. Write it all by yourself.

If you want someone to interview you for your book, there are turn-key services available, but they range in cost from a few thousand to tens of thousands.

If you'd rather write the book yourself, but want professional guidance, services can range from a few hundred dollars to tens of thousands. There are also a ton of books and online courses that can help you, all of which vary in price from zero dollars to several thousand.

Ghostwriting, the most expensive option, will typically cost you at least $40,000—but it can sometimes cost over $100,000.

And of course, you can write it all on your own for free (but again, I do not recommend this option for entrepreneurs).

Ultimately, out of all aspects of producing a book, writing is the hardest cost to calculate because it's so personal. Not to mention, this is one area where price does NOT always equal quality.

Just remember that there is *always* a cost for writing your book, even if it's only the opportunity cost of your time.

Low Quality: n/a
Acceptable: n/a
High Quality: n/a
Best Possible: n/a

PUBLISHING COST: EDITING

Editing is easier to price than writing, but still not as straightforward as you might imagine. The problem is not just the difference in the quality of editors; the problem is in the wide variety of different types of editing.

For the purpose of this pricing, we'll assume we're talking about a full content edit, which is what most authors need after writing the rough draft of their manuscript.

Low Quality: Less than $1K
Acceptable: $2K–$4K
High Quality: $5K–$10K
Best Possible: $15K+

PUBLISHING COST: COPYEDITING

Copyediting is easy to find at a low price. The problem is that if you don't do it right, you'll look terrible.

When people find bad grammar or misspelled words in your book, they literally think that you're stupid—it's totally unfair and irrational, but true (think about it, you probably do it to authors as well). So make sure that you pay enough to have it done properly.

I personally recommend having at least 2 different copy editors review your work. The prices below reflect only one, so double whatever it is you use.

Copyediting costs are highly variable, but the amounts below reflect the total cost for a 35K-word book (based on hourly pay).

Low Quality: $300 ($20 hour)
Acceptable: $450 ($30 hour)
High Quality: $600 ($40)
Best Possible: $750 ($50 hour)

PUBLISHING COST: COPYWRITING

This is something that authors often forget about, but it's crucially important if you want people to actually buy the book. That's because the book description is a big part of the reader's buying decision—and copywriters can help you perfect it.

Low Quality: $5–$25
Acceptable: $25–$75
High Quality: $75–$100
Best Possible: $150–$300

PUBLISHING COST: AUTHOR PHOTO

This is another instance where going for the lowest price will hurt you.

Whether we like it or not, people judge us based on our appearances. You need to make sure your author photo looks good and sends the right signals.

Low Quality: $0–$99
Acceptable: $100–$300
High Quality: $350–$1,000
Best Possible: $1,500+

PUBLISHING COST: BOOK COVER

Your book cover is likely going to be the biggest cost you have for publishing. But again—people *do* judge a book by its cover, and you must get this right.

Low Quality: $100–$150
Acceptable: $200–$500
High Quality: $750–$1,500
Best Possible: $2,000+

PUBLISHING COST: BOOK INTERIOR

Book interior really only matters when you get it wrong. No one notices when you get it right (unless it's an exceptionally amazing design or something like that), so you don't need to go super expensive here. You just need to get it "not wrong."

Low Quality: $0–$500 (DIY software like Vellum is in the middle of this range)
Acceptable: $750–$1,000
High Quality: $1,500
Best Possible: $2,500+

PUBLISHING COST: BOOK PRINTING (POD/EBOOK)

There are 2 basic ways to print books: print on demand (POD) or commercial offset printing.

With print on demand, the printing costs for orders are pulled out of the royalties, so there's no up-front publishing cost.

Thus, anything you spend depends on the format. Services

like CreateSpace and Kindle Direct Publishing charge nothing to set up paperbacks. IngramSpark charges $49 for physical book (hardcover or paperback) setup and $25 for eBook setup. The quality for IngramSpark tends to be about the same as CreateSpace.

Low Quality: n/a
Acceptable: $0 and/or $25–$74
High Quality: n/a
Best Possible: n/a

PUBLISHING COST: BOOK PRINTING (OFFSET)

Offset printing is when the books are not printed on demand but instead run in large batches, which is necessary for high-quality hardcovers.

While these tend to be higher quality, they do cost much more, if for no other reason than the fact that you're paying for the printing of the book before it's done.

It's almost impossible to quote a price here without knowing the quantity of books you'll be ordering. For example, 1,000 books will usually cost you between $5 and $7 apiece, whereas if you print 5,000, the price goes down to around $3 each. For more than 10,000, the price often drops below $2.

Furthermore, not everyone needs a hardcover. For this

reason, I can't really include this in the cost of publishing. Just know that if you want high-quality hardcovers, then you'll have to spend money on printing the books.

Low Quality: n/a
Acceptable: n/a
High Quality: n/a
Best Possible: n/a

PUBLISHING COST: ISBN

Getting an ISBN—the 13-digit number above the barcode at the back of your book—is necessary but kind of a pain.

If you're just planning to publish an eBook, you technically don't need one. But even if you're publishing in a digital format, there are perks to having your own ISBN.

ISBNs are unique identifiers used by every party involved with ordering, listing, selling, and stocking your book.

Most booksellers, aside from eBook platforms (like Amazon's Kindle Store), require ISBNs. Without one, your book will be invisible to publishers, brick-and-mortar stores, libraries, online retailers, and other links in the supply chain.

You can get a free ISBN through services like CreateSpace or IngramSpark, but there are downsides. First, your book looks more self-published. Second, you'll limit your chances of a bookstore carrying your book, as many won't take books from CreateSpace. Third, free ISBNs are often untransferable, so you run the risk of ending up with several ISBNs for the same book.

When it comes to ISBNs, you often get what you pay for. Bowker, the official ISBN Agency for publishers in the United States and its territories, has ISBNs available at $125.

Low Quality: $0
Acceptable: $85–$99
High Quality: $125
Best Possible: $125

TOTAL PUBLISHING COST

Low Quality: $2,000
Acceptable: $5,000
High Quality: $13,000
Best Possible: $18,000

This is not a true total cost, because writing help and hardcover publishing is *not* included. But looking at these general totals will help you understand what ranges you're looking at when considering publishing costs.

While it's important to know the up-front costs, keep your

ultimate objectives in mind when considering the total value of your book.

Books are the most powerful way to expedite and expand your career as an entrepreneur—if they're done the right way. Your ROI (both tangible and intangible) will be considerably greater if you make the proper investment up front.

SUMMARY

1. WHY ENTREPRENEURS SHOULD PROFESSIONALLY PUBLISH

You need to use a professional to publish your book for you. Professional publishing means paying a high-level professional to do everything for you so your book looks and feels great. Doing it yourself is a mess and makes you look bad. At a minimum, a high-quality professional publishing firm can help you with the following:

1. Manuscript evaluation and quality assurance
2. Book cover design
3. Interior layout
4. Printing and distribution

2. WHY ENTREPRENEURS SHOULD AVOID TRADITIONAL PUBLISHING

Traditional publishing is usually a bad choice for entrepreneurs because:

1. It's extremely difficult to get a traditional publishing deal.
2. You'll have no ownership of rights and profits.
3. You lose creative and content control.
4. You lose marketing control (and get no support).
5. It's a huge time investment.

3. WHAT MAKES A BOOK PROFESSIONALLY PUBLISHED?

1. The title
2. The recommending source
3. The cover
4. The book description
5. The blurbs (aka endorsements)
6. The customer reviews
7. The author bio and picture (depending on where the picture is placed)
8. The length of the book
9. The price (though this can come sooner)
10. The book text itself (the "Look Inside" function online)

4. WHAT DOES IT COST TO PROFESSIONALLY PUBLISH?

A book is one of the most valuable assets you can invest in as an entrepreneur, which is why it's important to hire knowledgeable professionals to ensure a high-quality product.

It can cost upwards of $20,000 to publish a book on your own, and this does not take into account the time and opportunity costs associated with figuring out a process you've never done before with little outside help.

Investing that money up front in a firm that specializes in writing, editing, and publishing books maximizes that investment, ensures that the final book will be something worthy of your reputation, and allows you to focus on your core competencies. Your ROI (both tangible and intangible) will be considerably greater if you make the proper investment up front.

CONCLUSION

GET STARTED NOW, GET YOUR BIG PAYOFF SOON

I was very clear about the point of this book: **to convince every entrepreneur to write their book.**

The reasons to write a book are overwhelming:

PRESTIGE/BRAND PAYOFFS

Your book establishes your authority and raises your prestige in many ways:

1. Levels up your identity (you're an author)
2. Positions you in the world
3. Increases your visibility and raises your profile
4. Establishes your authority and credibility

BUSINESS PAYOFFS

Your book helps your business in many ways:

1. Is the perfect 24/7 salesperson
2. Reduces your risk to others and facilitates word of mouth
3. Gets you new clients and opportunities
4. Recruits top-tier talent for your business

IMPACT ON OTHERS PAYOFFS

Your book impacts others in many ways:

1. Helps people
2. Scales your impact
3. Improves your family relationships

PERSONAL GROWTH PAYOFFS

Your book helps you grow as a person in many ways:

1. Gives you confidence and pride of accomplishment
2. Gives you creative expression
3. Creates self-improvement and skill development
4. Helps you escape from your idea
5. Shows intentionality

LEGACY PAYOFFS

Your book helps you leave something behind for others in many ways:

1. Helps you leave a legacy
2. Provides future intellectual capital
3. Is proof of impact and existence

Once you've decided to try it, you next need to sell yourself on writing it. Ask yourself: ***Why do I want to write this book?*** There are 2 ways to answer this question:

STEP 1: WHY ARE YOU WRITING YOUR BOOK?

1. The Bean Counter Answer: What exactly will you get from writing a book?

This is usually the quantifiable stuff, what to tell your CFO to convince them to let you spend the money to write this book—things like money, prestige, business, visibility, etc.

2. The Deeper Answer: What's the real reason writing a book appeals to you?

This is usually the harder-to-measure stuff, but that matters a lot—things like legacy, personal growth, relationships, impact, and purpose.

STEP 2: FIGURE OUT WHO WILL CARE

3. Who's the ideal reader for your book?

This is about who your book is written for. In essence, *who do you want to be a hero to?*

4. Why will they care?

Now you have to understand why they're going to care about your book. *How can your knowledge help someone solve a problem or create a transformation in their life?*

STEP 3: FIND THE OBSTACLES AND FLIP THEM

5. Why haven't you written your book yet?

This is about understanding what has held you back in the past, so you can ensure that you avoid or solve that problem this time and get your book done.

6. What's your plan?

How will you overcome these obstacles and challenges?

STEP 4: CLOSING THE SALE

7. Worst Result?

What if you don't write your book? What happens to you (and your readers)?

8. Best Result?

What if you do write your book? What happens to you (and your readers)?

ANSWERING THE OBJECTIONS

For most entrepreneurs—probably 97%—the idea of writing a book immediately undermines their confidence. So how do you solve it?

1. Write only about what fascinates and motivates you.
1. Write only to those you need and those who can use your help.
2. Write only about something you've already been paid for.
3. Give a recipe for successful change.
4. Spend money to make time.

Outlining a book can be simple for an entrepreneur if you use this fast method, which is designed to take no more than 30 minutes.

THE 30-MINUTE BOOK OUTLINE

STEP 1: BRAINSTORM THE CHAPTERS FOR YOUR BOOK (10-MINUTE TIME LIMIT)

The first step in creating your outline is to brainstorm what chapters go in your book. Spend no more than 10 minutes on this.

STEP 2: CREATE A TABLE OF CONTENTS (5-MINUTE TIME LIMIT)

Once you've brainstormed your chapters, put them in your Table of Contents, and write the key takeaway for each chapter. This is called a thesis statement.

A thesis statement is a short summation of the main point you want to make in the chapter. *Do not* overwrite these. They should be 1 or 2 sentences each—that's it.

STEP 3: PUT IN THE CHAPTER CONTENTS (15-MINUTE TIME LIMIT)

Using the Table of Contents you created, fill in the content for each chapter. You are filling in the main points and stories and examples in your book, and that's it.

Once your book is outlined, there are 4 ways to write your book:

1. Have someone interview you to get your content, but they write it.

Most entrepreneurs should do this. It's the quickest, best way to ensure that your book is good and that it gets done with the least amount of effort from you.

2. Write it yourself, with professional guidance.

This works as well; it just takes more time and effort, but can be worth the cost to some entrepreneurs.

3. Hire a ghostwriter and have them write it.

This can work but can be a bit sketchy, because of specific problems with ghostwriters.

4. Write it all by yourself.

This is the worst choice by far.

Once you have your book written, then you need to professionally publish it.

1. Why Entrepreneurs Should Professionally Publish

You need to use a professional to publish your book for you. Professional publishing means paying a high-level professional to do everything for you so your book looks and feels great. Doing it yourself is a mess and makes you look bad. At a minimum, a high-quality professional publishing firm can help you with the following:

1. Manuscript evaluation and quality assurance
2. Book cover design
3. Interior layout

4. Printing and distribution

2. *Why Entrepreneurs Should Avoid Traditional Publishing*

Traditional publishing is usually a bad choice for entrepreneurs because:

1. It's extremely difficult to get a traditional publishing deal
2. You'll have no ownership of rights and profits
3. You lose creative and content control
4. You lose marketing control (and get no support)
5. It's a huge time investment

3. *What Makes a Book Professionally Published?*

1. The title
2. The recommending source
3. The cover
4. The book description
5. The blurbs (aka endorsements)
6. The customer reviews
7. The author bio and picture (depending on where the picture is placed)
8. The length of the book
9. The price (though this can come sooner)
10. The book text itself (the "Look Inside" function online)

4. What Does It Cost to Professionally Publish?

A book is one of the most valuable assets you can invest in as an entrepreneur, which is why it's important to hire knowledgeable professionals to ensure a high-quality product.

It can cost upwards of $20,000 to publish a book on your own, and this does not take into account the time and opportunity costs associated with figuring out a process you've never done before with little outside help.

Investing that money up front in a firm that specializes in writing, editing, and publishing books maximizes that investment, ensures that the final book will be something worthy of your reputation, and allows you to focus on your core competencies. Your ROI (both tangible and intangible) will be considerably greater if you make the proper investment up front.

If you need any other help beyond what's in here, there are 2 things you can do:

1. Go to ScribeBookSchool.com. That site details our entire book writing process. There is no catch—it's all free. Literally everything we do as a service, we teach for free. Obviously my company has a load of paid services, but the information is all free.
2. Email me and ask: tucker@scribemedia.com. That is my real email. I'm happy to help out in any way you need.

There's not much else Dan and I can do beyond this. Either you get it, or you don't.

If you don't, that's fine.

But if you do, then I'm excited to soon welcome you to the author club and read your book!

ABOUT THE AUTHORS

DAN SULLIVAN

Dan Sullivan is the world's foremost expert on entrepreneurship and has coached more successful entrepreneurs than anyone on the planet. He is the co-founder of Strategic Coach®, the leading entrepreneurial coaching program in the world, and the author of more than 50 publications on entrepreneurial success. Over the past 30+ years, Strategic Coach has provided teaching and training to more than 20,000 entrepreneurs. www.strategiccoach.com

TUCKER MAX

Tucker Max is the co-founder of Scribe Media, a company that helps people write, publish, and market their books. He has written four *New York Times* bestsellers, which have sold over 4.5 million copies worldwide. He currently lives in Austin, Texas, with his wife, Veronica, and three children.